JOURNAL OF
Museum Education
A PUBLICATION OF THE MUSEUM EDUCATION ROUNDTABLE

VOLUME 37 · NUMBER 3 · FALL 2012

Museum Education in Times of Radical Social Change

ents continues on page 2

;BN 978-1-61132-821-9

ISSN 1059–8650

D1352803

Cover: Sarajevo artist Nusret Pašić's work symbolically illustrates the content of the guest-edited section of this issue. The deformed human head, standing behind the bars preventing passage towards progress, is caught in the act of screaming in desperation. It appears to be trying to raise the human spirit above everyday reality and overcome the post-war crisis in Bosnia and Herzegovina, illustrated through the background of daily newspapers. With this work Pašić joined other local and international artists and architect Renzo Piano to create the Ars Aevi Museum of Contemporary Art in Sarajevo, which now awaits its permanent home. This new museum has a potential to participate in the socio-political renewal of the devastated country through public and educational reforms.

JOURNAL OF
Museum Education
A PUBLICATION OF THE MUSEUM EDUCATION ROUNDTABLE

Editors-in-Chief

TINA R. NOLAN, Ed.D
President, Tina Nolan Consulting

CYNTHIA ROBINSON
Director of Museum Studies, Tufts University

Museum Education in Times of Radical Social Change

The *Museum Education Roundtable* (MER) is a nonprofit organization based in Washington DC, dedicated to enriching and promoting the field of museum education. Through publications, programs, and communication networks, MER fosters professionalism, encourages leadership, scholarship, and research in museum-based learning, and advocates for the inclusion and application of museum-based learning in the general education arena. For more information on MER and its activities, please visit the MER website at www.museumeducation.info and click on 'contact us.' MER members receive the *Journal of Museum Education* as a benefit of membership. To join MER, visit the website at www.museumeducation.info or write to MER at PO Box 15727, Washington, DC 20003.

First published 2012 by Museum Education Roundtable

Published 2016 by Routledge
2 Park Square, Milton Park, Abingdon, Oxon OX14 4RN
711 Third Avenue, New York, NY 10017, USA

Routledge is an imprint of the Taylor & Francis Group, an informa business

Production and Composition by Detta Penna and Adriane Bosworth

ISBN 13: 978-1-611-32821-9 (pbk)

Tina R. Nolan and Cynthia Robinson

Winter 2011: Madison, Wisconsin

Tens of thousands of public service employees from across the State of Wisconsin descended on the capitol to protest Governor Scott Walker's plan to remove collective bargaining rights for unionized state workers. Governor Walker argued that this provision in his budget was necessary to close a massive budget gap, brought about by the 2008 financial meltdown that led to the current recession. As many as 100,000 teachers, police officers, factory workers, firemen, and nurses left their homes and families to march on the capitol square and camp in the capitol rotunda. Together they implored the governor to reconsider his plan. At the same time, supporters of the governor's plan were mobilizing, making their way to the capitol to argue in favor of its implementation. Everyday life in the state had become contentious: Neighbors argued with neighbors, lifelong friendships ended, and public service employees faced vocal opposition in such unlikely places as their local grocery stores and restaurants. Students in classrooms asked their teachers to talk about what was happening — clearly a teachable moment and an opportunity to discuss democracy and civic dialogue, but union rules prohibited teachers from discussing any aspect of the conflict while on school property.[1]

Feeling compelled to join the protest, I made my way to Madison from my home in Chicago. When I arrived I noticed, among the throngs of protesters, that several museums were located next to the capitol square. Were any museum educators standing alongside their fellow Wisconsin schoolteachers, marching in solidarity with them for teachers' rights to bargain for salary, class size, and proper resources for public schools? After all, significant cuts to public education would have direct implications for museums and ultimately for museum workers. Consider this example: Less money for public schools means larger class sizes, fewer teachers, and a narrowed curriculum. A narrowed curriculum means less priority given to non-core subject areas like history, geography, and the arts. It also means fewer resources allocated for school field trips and outreach programs for schools — particularly those programs in non-core subject areas. Fewer teachers in public schools mean a drop in attendance for teacher professional development workshops provided by museums. A drop in attendance for school

Journal of Museum Education, Volume 37, Number 3, Fall 2012, pp. 5–8.

Teachers and other public service workers from throughout the state of Wisconsin protesting at the state capitol in March, 2011.
Photo by Mark Larson, Ed.D.

field trips, outreach visits to classrooms, and teacher workshops means a drop in revenue for museums. And a loss of revenue in museums means that museums must tighten their belts. When museums cut budgets, museum workers lose their jobs.

When I returned to Chicago, I contacted some Wisconsin museum educators, looking to invite them to attend discussion and support groups for teachers in the wake of the protests. While in conversation with one museum educator, I asked, "What has it been like for you, to be smack-dab in the middle of this ongoing and massive public protest?"

"Well," the educator said, "the numbers of visitors to the museum has really dropped."

"Have you participated in the public demonstrations in any way?" I asked.

"I see the protesters every day, but, no, I haven't taken part in the protest."

Granted, this was only one exchange with one person, and it's an easy strategy to extrapolate out for the sake of making a point. It's entirely possible that other museum educators in the area were marching alongside their fellow teachers, and that still others had joined the hundreds of local protest marches organized across the state. But this exchange did give me pause. Why was this educator so removed from what was happening all over? Did this person fear taking a side in such a contentious debate? Were they instructed not to participate by museum leadership? Did this person not understand the potential implications that eliminating collective bargaining rights would bring? Did this educator feel ancillary to the public education system and not a direct part of it? Do other museum educators feel the same way? Are museum educators ready to take part in educational change efforts by actively involving themselves in the politics of education?

Ready or not, we are in a period of massive changes to systems set-up in the 20th century. The systems that worked in the Industrial Age (financial, educational, etc.) simply do not function in the global and networked Knowledge Age in which we currently operate. The world's financial system will not return to its previous state. In the United States, there will be fewer federal and state dollars available to support the work of cultural institutions, and philanthropic giving will not look as it did during the 1990s. Our public education system, currently broken, will not be fixed, but will instead evolve into something quite different than what we experienced as students. As museum professionals, we have several questions to ask ourselves. Chief among them: What will the role of museums be in twenty-five years and how will museums sustain themselves? What role will museum educators play in the evolution of our public education system?

In this issue of the *JME*, we hear from museum professionals in the midst of navigating large socio-political changes across the globe. Guest Editors Asja Mandić and Patrick Roberts have gathered the voices and experiences of museum professionals from Albania, Bosnia and Herzegovina, Hungary, Israel, Kosovo, Macedonia, Montenegro, Serbia, and Slovenia. Together they examine museum education practices and museum operations in post-conflict societies. Elizabeth Merritt, Founding Director of AAM's Center for the Future of Museums, roots her article in the latest research about demographic, educational, political, economic, and environmental trends, and gives readers an opportunity to imagine how museum educators in this country might weather dramatic systemic shifts and lead change.

True to form with past *JME*s, readers will also find articles dedicated to articulating the most current practices in our field. Scott Pattison and Lynn Dierking disseminate their latest research about staff facilitation of family activities. Madeline Karp shares a case study of her experience making outreach crafts meaningful. Nora Moynihan and Betsy Diamant-Cohen discuss ways to create preschool programming in exhibit spaces intended for free play, and Jayne Gordon reviews the latest literature about collaborative online learning.

Our aim is to create shared language and practice among the educators in our field. The guest-edited section in this issue shines an international light on museum educators navigating tumultuous change, and we hope that museum educators in the United States will learn from the experiences of their overseas peers.

Taken as a whole, this issue models the framework of a successful change process: One starts by articulating the details of how things are done in the present, including an analysis of the systems that support how things are done. One creates a vision of how things can be done in the future, and either fixes old or creates new systems to support the new vision. And one builds a bridge between the old and the new; a roadmap of sorts for the profession. The theory is simple, but as you'll see from our authors, the practice is very, very hard.

Museum educators are the driving force behind the content of the *JME*, and to that end Cynthia and I hope you will consider writing for a future issue. Guidelines for single manuscript submissions and guest editor proposals can be found on both the Left Coast Press web site at www.lcoastpress.com and the Museum Education Roundtable web site at www.museumeducation.info. Single articles and guest editor proposals are accepted on an ongoing basis.

We welcome your submissions and look forward to expanding the conversation and contributions to the museum education literature through the *JME*. Should you need to speak with me or Cynthia, please email us at JMuseEd@ gmail.com.   — Tina

Notes

1. In April of 2011, I conducted a focus group with Wisconsin educators to learn what their daily lives were like in the wake of the protests. These educators were faculty members from National Louis University's Wisconsin campus where they taught graduate programs for schoolteachers. Using class time as a means for providing a safe place to discuss the political events, and as a way to discuss school finance, progressive unionism, and politics, these faculty shared with me the direct experiences of the classroom teachers in their graduate classes. For more information about this moment in Wisconsin state history, see the Wisconsin State Journal and the Milwaukee Journal Sentinel archives:
http://host.madison.com/wsj/
http://www.jsonline.com/.

About the Editors-in-Chief

Dr. Tina Nolan, Co-Editor-in-Chief of the *JME*, is the principal of Tina Nolan Consulting, an education consulting group (www.tinanolan.com). She has over 18 years experience working in museums in Chicago including Brookfield Zoo, Lincoln Park Zoo and the Peggy Notebaert Nature Museum where she served as Director of Education. Dr. Nolan works nationally and internationally with museums and other not-for-profit educational organizations as an independent education consultant, researcher, guest lecturer, and writer.

Cynthia Robinson, Co-Editor-in-Chief of the *JME*, is the director of museum studies at Tufts University. She spent 25 years working in and with museums, and has extensive experience in developing programs, curricula, and exhibitions, as well as in museum management and administration.

Museum Education in Times of Radical Social Change

International Perspectives and Problems

Asja Mandić and Patrick Roberts

Introduction

Museum educators in the United States and Canada are no strangers to controversy and challenge: tight budgets and limited resources, economic recession, the politics of cultural heritage and exhibition development, debates over public value and accessibility, and the challenge to remain relevant in a media saturated world. Challenges such as these engage the attention of museum workers around the globe daily. Yet many international museum professionals also contend with challenges far beyond the experiences of most US or Canadian museums. How does a museum survive the transition from communism to capitalism? How does a museum survive war and the collapse of a nation? How are museum partnerships built among former wartime enemies? What challenges do museum educators face in post-conflict societies? And perhaps more importantly, how are such challenges met?

This issue of *JME* explores the ways in which museums in zones of conflict and regions marked by radical and rapid socio-political change perform their public service role and educational mission. Through a rich variety of museum concepts and practices shaped by local/national/regional histories, contexts, and dilemmas, readers are introduced to educational activities in nine countries that have witnessed dramatic social change and/or violent conflict over the last few decades — Albania, Bosnia and Herzegovina, Hungary, Israel, Kosovo, Macedonia, Montenegro, Serbia, and Slovenia.

Perhaps the most radical examples of how museums experience socio-political transition and post-conflict recovery followed by the economic recession are found in the case of Bosnia and Herzegovina, where Asja is a professor of art

Journal of Museum Education, Volume 37, Number 3, Fall 2012, pp. 9–14.

history at the University of Sarajevo and where Patrick spent five months studying museum education. With the collapse of socialist Yugoslavia in 1991, the newly independent Bosnia and Herzegovina suffered a tragic war that killed more than a hundred thousand people and displaced millions. The capital city of Sarajevo, home to a variety of well-established museums, suffered a terrible siege that left more than 10,000 dead. By the time the Dayton Peace Accords ended the war in 1995, Sarajevo, its people, and its museums had endured tremendous devastation. In establishing the foundations for Bosnia's complicated post-war government, the Dayton Accords failed to address the legal status of national museums, and this has resulted in scarce or non-existent funding for even the most basic of museum functions — paying the utility bills and paying the staff — and a limited ability to apply for non-governmental funding. This dire financial crisis has forced some museums in Sarajevo to close their doors to the public, such as the Art Gallery of Bosnia and Herzegovina which closed in September 2011.

How might international perspectives inform our work as museum professionals working in the more stable social and cultural settings? We believe that deepened understanding of the challenges associated with this work can help museum educators in the US better articulate a case for how museum education is necessary for and vitally important to the health of a democratic society. We believe museum professionals everywhere can benefit from learning how dedicated, creative museum educators working in difficult environments (re)adjust to new circumstances and overcome obstacles that may be inconceivable to some readers. We also hope these articles will spark information-sharing across international boundaries and encourage international partnerships and collaborative exchanges.

Overview

This issue represents a collection of individual voices rather than common authorial narrative. By inviting scholars and specialists from different museum-related disciplines and backgrounds, those who have direct experience working in or with museums, we opted to present a range of perspectives on the topic of museum education and to identify broader questions and concerns facing museums in the contemporary world. The contributors discuss the educational function of very different museum institutions — varying in terms of size, subject matter, management and funding arrangements, geographical and socio-political contexts — and sometimes education is understood in the broadest sense, through the practices demonstrating the museum's social role. The articles presented in this issue can be grouped into two categories: (1) those that examine museum education practices and museum functioning in times of dramatic social, political, and economic change, specifically the transition from socialist/ communist to capitalist/democratic systems of governance; (2) those that analyze the specific educational and socially-oriented approaches of various museums and centers in recent war zones and areas of conflict.

The article by Tamás Vásárhelyi of the Hungarian Natural History Museum provides an historical overview of museum education in Hungary and describes relationships and tensions between past practices and more recent projects, i.e., how past approaches are rearticulated or set aside in current museum practices. He leads us through the story of museum growth and development in his country in a way that reflects the complexity of European history, for example the rise and fall of the Austro-Hungarian Empire, the effects of the World Wars, the consequences of the Cold War and Soviet domination, and freedom of the country that was, for several decades, isolated by the so-called Iron Curtain from the rest of the world. Throughout Vásárhelyi's article, we get a comparative sense of how museums functioned under two different political and economic systems: On the one hand, the centralization of the museum system and control of museum programs and exhibition content by the Communist party, and on the other hand, the paradox of democratic freedom, in which institutions lost the full support of the state or municipality and entered into a highly competitive cultural market. For museums, this transition towards a free democratic state marked the beginning of a period of financial instability that had a particular effect on museum education. However, his examination of the most recent museum approaches reflects significant changes in the ways museums perceive their relationship towards the public in terms of visitor services and educational programming.

Adela Železnik, the author of the second article, also reflects upon the transition from a communist system to democracy through the example of the Museum of Modern Art (Moderna galerija) in Ljubljana, the capital of Slovenia. Formerly one of the six republics that made up the socialist Yugoslavia, Slovenia, like Bosnia and Herzegovina, became an independent country with the collapse of Yugoslavia in 1991. Unlike Hungary, which was under the control of the Soviet Union, Yugoslavia had a more open society in which citizens could travel freely and where Western influence was not tightly controlled. As a result, artists enjoyed more creative freedom; hence contemporary art in the socialist Yugoslavia was closer to Western models than to other socialist countries. For Železnik, understanding the socialist doctrine in the context of the educational frameworks and programs of the past becomes essential in examining the current programming strategies in Slovenia.

The authors of our third and fourth articles, Diana Walters and Ziva Haller Rubenstein, write about museums in regions of conflict. In illustrating the role museums and arts-based institutions can play in overcoming geographic, national, ethnic and religious borders and conflicts, each article suggests new perspectives on thinking about the challenges and opportunities offered by collaborative projects that work to establish a common platform for defining concepts, content, target groups, objectives, and educational approaches.

Diana Walters provides a valuable perspective as the only "outsider" among this issue's contributors in that she is a museum professional who is not native to the region she discusses. She describes the challenges of coordinating a collaborative project among eleven museum institutions from six different Balkan countries. The countries involved in her project are still going through the process of transition (from communism/socialism to capitalism/democracy) and all of them (except for Albania) witnessed the collapse of their common state, the Socialist Federal Republic of Yugoslavia, and became independent. It is important to emphasize that her role as a leader in the project required mediation between nations recently at war with one another: Bosnia and Herzegovina; Kosovo, where US troops had to intervene in the conflict between Serbs and Kosovo Albanians; Serbia and Montenegro, which were directly involved in aggression against Bosnia and Herzegovina. The project Walters describes was directed towards initiating more socially-oriented, inclusive dialogical approaches to exhibition development and educational programming, with the potential of leading towards conflict resolution in the Balkan region. Walters's examination is particularly significant for building awareness of the social role and function of museum institutions and their need to engage in more inclusive approaches in relation to their publics — to focus more on their educational function and potential to contribute to the learning process, which can be viewed as a significant strategy in improving the image of museum institutions in the region.

Writing from Israel, Ziva Haller Rubenstein adds significantly to discussions on the ability of cultural institutions to generate social and political improvements, especially in the realm of conflict remediation. Haller Rubenstein's study of the Centre for Digital Art in Holon, Israel, highlights the centre's ability to be responsive to community needs and to be engaged in social service activities. Throughout the description of the centre's efforts to understand the needs of its immediate social surroundings and audiences, Haller Rubenstein shows how the centre develops community-oriented and art mediation activities that lead to the empowerment of marginal and disempowered social groups and which actively involve open, dialogical processes about burning political issues. In striving for these goals, the Centre for Digital Art in Holon goes far beyond what other museums in Israel have achieved. Haller Rubenstein's essay provides a significant contribution to understanding the importance of a social orientation of museum functioning and its potential to transform modes of thinking and perceptions of contemporary Israeli society. Her contribution not only highlights the potential value of creating hybrid museum practices responsive to particular socio-political settings, but it also raises questions about the tension between an art museum's institutional responsibility and its social responsibility.

Conclusion

Museum educators in the United States currently face difficult programming and funding decisions brought about by economic uncertainty and political change. At almost every level, museum workers, particularly educators, must make the case for their own social relevance and public value. Why are robust museum education programs important to democratic life? What can they contribute to reconciliation between opposing points of view? How can they promote civic pluralism? Why is it even necessary that they do so? By giving voice to international perspectives on questions such as these, we hope this issue of *JME* will help inspire and facilitate a global conversation on the role museums must play in promoting peace, reconciliation, civic pluralism, and democratic citizenship.

About the Authors

Asja Mandić is assistant professor in the Art History Department, University of Sarajevo, teaching courses in modern and contemporary art and museum studies at both the undergraduate and graduate levels. She worked as a curator of the Ars Aevi Museum of Contemporary Art, Sarajevo. She curated over twenty exhibitions, edited a book, *ArteFacts* (Sarajevo: Ars Aevi, 2007), and is the author of five exhibition catalogues.

Patrick Roberts is associate professor at National-Louis University, in the Department of Educational Foundations and Inquiry. Dr. Roberts is a recent Fulbright Scholar who studied museum education in Bosnia and Herzegovina and the Western Balkans. He is the former Director of Education at the Museum of Broadcast Communications in Chicago.

The Hungarian Patient

Museum Education in Hungary and the Challenges of Democratic Transition

Tamás Vásárhelyi

Abstract   This article outlines the changes, developments, activities, and challenges faced by Hungarian museums over the last few decades. It shows that there was life behind the "Iron Curtain," with museums enjoying relative financial stability. While the political and economic changes associated with the transition from a communist to a democratically elected government and capitalist economy did bring more international connections, collaborations, and freedom in choosing exhibition topics, the changes also brought exposure to the harsh rules of the cultural market. This article reflects on these issues and presents some of the most recent museum approaches in terms of programming, education, and audience development.

Located in Central Europe, Hungary is a relatively small country (approximately the size of West Virginia) with a population of ten million people. From 1949 to 1989, Hungary was known as the Hungarian Socialist People's Republic, a communist country closely aligned with the Soviet Union and a member of the Warsaw Pact. In 1989, it became a developing democracy, with free elections and a capitalist economy. The initial enthusiasm that came with democratic transition later gave way to cautiousness and even skepticism as the country underwent the good and bad experiences of "freedom." Today, the differences between rich and poor are greater than during the socialist past, and recently, due to the worldwide economic crisis and the state of the Hungarian economy,[1] the majority of Hungarians fear the precarious financial situation. These political and economic changes, as well as changes in cultural policy and the cultural habits and attidtudes of audiences, have a significant impact on museums.

Journal of Museum Education, Volume 37, Number 3, Fall 2012, pp. 15–30.

A Glorious Past

The history of public museums in Hungary can be traced to the early 19th century, when Ferenc Széchényi, an enlightened Hungarian count, laid the foundation for Hungary's National Museum by donating to his country 13,000 books, maps, drawings, paintings, coins, and old curiosities. This donation established the world's third national public collection. Exhibitions in those times were not especially constructed as a means of communication. Apart from larger fine art pieces, the museum collection was preserved in cases and drawers, and the nicest pieces were exhibited in glass-walled cases and glass-covered drawers. Objects were shown in their classificatory system and accompanied by name and catalogue data only. On special days, the museum offered free admission to the general public. Growing national consciousness and patriotic feelings prompted people, rich and poor alike, to donate curiosities, objects, and collections to the National Museum, while state support and financial donations made systematic acquisitions possible.

At the turn of the 19th century, Hungary celebrated the millennial anniversary of the arrival of ethnic Hungarians to the Carpathian Basin. This period was the golden age of modern Hungary, and many local communities established their own city museums with great ambition and a belief that museums play a significant role in cultural development, identity formation and self-representation. In Hungary there were about a hundred museums at the turn of the century.

The largest museum in the country: The Hungarian National Museum.

One of the smallest museums in the country, in Bükkzsérc: the local history exhibition is made by local enthusiasts.

As a consequence of its defeat in World War I, Hungary lost two-thirds of its territory. A lack of natural resources and a damaged industry weakened the economy, and the country could no longer develop its museum system, maintaining it only through great effort.[2]

Post-World War II

Following World War II, Hungary became a socialist, or communist country. The Party ruled the economy as well as everyday life. Hungarian society was split between those who supported this system and those who did not (and consequently had to hide their views, especially in the first decades of socialist rule). The existence of public institutions depended, directly or indirectly, almost entirely on the Party.

The rapid growth of museums in post-war Hungary paralleled much of the rest of the world. While in 1958 there were 89 museums in the country, this number grew to 538 by 1982, and to over 800 by 2000. By no means was this development supported with appropriate building activity. By 1980, only one museum building had been erected; all other museums existed in old monuments, abandoned schools, and other community buildings, often without the necessary conditions for the preservation and care of objects or for public services.

During the socialist regime the museum system in Hungary was increasingly centralized. Many private collections were expropriated and turned into state property (i.e., were integrated into public museum collections). The National Centre for Museums and Monuments provided regular support and evaluation. Museums were expected, as a comrade wrote in 1952, "to support the success of the cultural revolution, and the fight of our party, in forming the mind of workers, and socialist men." In 1976, the new Five-Year Plan for museums stated as one of its objectives that "museums become multiple public educational places, with higher standards of acquisitions and research and that they have to provide useful knowledge and entertainment to all segments of the society, especially the workers and the youth."[3] There were expectations of appropriate political and ideological topics of exhibitions, but, at least in the field of natural history, these did not go much further than mirroring Darwinism and declaring the superiority of Soviet science. A new national museum was established for the history of the labor movement.[4]

In the 1960s and 1970s, the Hungarian government turned state ownership of local museums over to community-based councils called "soviets." These soviets supported museums financially, hired museum professionals, approved plans, and monitored results. A museum Inspectorate was established in which the inspectors were members of one of the fourteen, academically different national museums.[5]

The shift of museums from science and research-centered institutions towards audience-centered, educational, and later even recreational institutions emphasized by the International Council of Museums (ICOM)[6] in the 1960s and 1970s soon reached Hungarian museums. First a party decree, then the Public Education Law (1976) ordered museums to establish education departments, and broaden their educational activities in the form of new, didactic exhibitions, new series of lectures, and meetings with members and groups of "the worker class." A holdover from of this period may still be seen in Szombathely.

The governmental pressure on education was not well received by curators and museum directors (most often once curators themselves). Resistance developed against the forced changes and against the new "educational" colleagues who had no degree in the academic field of the museum (for example, ethnography, biology, history, or art history) and sometimes were even considered "propagandists." Even today, many Hungarian curators and museum directors still do not accept fully that education is as much a discipline as any other scientific field. If we may speak of a "pecking order" in museums, educators certainly are most often on the lower end. This shared conscience may have helped museum

A relic of the seventies: An old fashioned archaeological exhibition in 2009, at Szombathely.

educators across the country work in hidden and informal networks, with empathy and sympathy towards each other. In any event, graduate educators were employed by many museums. Their in-service training was organized by the Central Museum Directorate (CMD), and it was supported by a series of publications and translations of various museum-related papers and resolutions from the democratic part of the world and from organizations like ICOM.

In a way, these were peaceful decades; society and government made no extra demands. Entrance fees were low and museums were uninterested in the revenue. Although they were poorly funded, they were fully supported by the state or municipality. Due to the efforts of museum educators, systematic work began in audience development, which had an impact on visitor numbers, too.

The accompanying graph shows the number of total annual visitors to Hungarian museums over the last four decades. Attendance is a consequence of the total number and performance of the museums of Hungary, but it also is a conse-

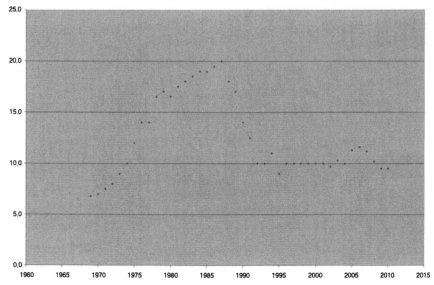

A museum "fever-curve:" The change in the total annual number of visitors to all Hungarian museums over the last 4 decades. Figures for this graph are the results of both old and more recent data mining in published or unpublished official statistics.

quence of economic, political, and social changes, as well as the effects of the development of the cultural market and the leisure time industry. The total number of visitors to all Hungarian museums rose rapidly in the sixties and seventies, reaching a maximum of twenty million a year (about twice the population of the country). The growing numbers in those decades were the result of limited cultural choice and the forced education wave of the sixties and seventies. Thousands of tourist buses brought visitors with low expectations towards exhibitions from neighboring socialist countries. Socialist brigades, consisting of employees working in the same unit of a factory were directed to regularly visit cultural events and institutions. (There are anecdotes about a lone brigade member arriving at the museum and buying a dozen tickets to be glued into the logbook of the brigade while the other brigade members had a nice time in a pub.)

Visitor numbers began to decrease not when the first serious economic problems arrived (rising living costs and rising entrance fees, starting around 1978), but in the late 1980s, when citizens were allowed to travel more freely to Western countries and visit better museum exhibitions. Greater television, video, and movie choices also contributed to the drop off in museum attendance. Thus, a real cultural market came into existence. Fewer expenditures on culture and rising fees paralleled rising visitor expectations and competition for leisure time. In 2000, attendance seemed to stabilize at around ten million visitors (the population of the country). The reasons for the increase and then dip a couple of years ago will be explained later.

In the 1980s, the power of the Party began to erode, with economic difficulties paralleling growing social and political tensions. As a response to the decrease in public support, several museums eliminated educational activities, education staff, and even whole departments so as to spend the given money "to save the collections" (instead of increasing the income or looking for another solution).[7] The Central Museum Directorate was eliminated, and no training or help was given to museum educators. Some "spiritual" workshops still endured with great efforts of a few loyal and enthusiastic educators.[8]

Transition into a Free Democratic State[9]

With the political and economic changes that accompanied the collapse of Hungary's socialist system of government, property that had belonged to the local soviet councils became the responsibility of local governments. The new, democratically elected government provided a budget for the promotion of culture that local governments allocated to a variety of cultural activities and institutions, including libraries and museums. Increased travel opportunities, international experience, and expertise played a significant role in modernizing Hungarian museology and museum education.[10]

Democracy brought relative freedom to the museum community in such areas as the establishment of civic societies, no government pressure in selecting the topic of exhibitions, and an application system for higher rank museum managers (with less and no one-party political pressure on the selection process). Very few propaganda-driven museums were closed around the political changes. The number of museums was continuously (although slowly) growing while visitor numbers fell.

The Pulszky Society-Hungarian Museum Association was established in 1989, and its first and the most active group was the education division, which organized meetings, conferences, and publications. The Hungarian Society for Environmental Education, in partnership with the Hungarian Natural History Museum, started to work with museums in 1992 and established its own Museum Group in 1995. Conferences and training, like School in the Museum (1998), Museum in the School (2000), and publications show the enthusiasm and devotedness of these years. The Dutch Museum Association provided great help in modernizing museum management in Hungary, with a series of museum management trainings from 1992 onward. Beyond acknowledging new management methods, Hungarian participants of the management courses who were used to functioning on safe, government support, were surprised that visitors, audience, and stakeholders should be given so much attention. Museum directors repeatedly visited Dutch museums, and another group enjoyed an International Visitor Program in the US. Travel grants were more easily available to all, and foreign museum directors and curators visited Hungary in numbers never before seen. Hungarians became more active in ICOM committees and in the European Museum Forum.

Towards the Visitor-Friendly Museum

The new social demands affected museum architecture in Hungary in the 1990s. Existing institutions were reconstructed (for example, the Hungarian National Museum and the Museum of Fine Arts), followed by the development or renewal of up-to-date visitor spaces and infrastructure. New museum buildings (Ludwig Museum, Open Air Museum) were even erected.

In 2002, the government's cultural branch announced a museum strategy that included the improvement of visitor services. The so-called "Alpha Program" gave priority to defining conceptual directions in this area. Sub-projects focused on temporary exhibitions, accessibility and mobility, and also promoted a visitor-friendly attitude (and visitor-friendly spaces) in museums generally. Many museum buildings received new appearances and infrastructure through the Alpha Program as well. Parallel with this, another program, Museums for Everybody, was started. Free publications provided information about museum programs and offered help to teachers planning school visits.[11] Scientific studies were carried out that analyzed the expectations of Hungarians toward visitor-friendly museums, as well as visitor behavior.[12]

In order to improve the museums' relation to the public, new programs and awards were also conceived. The Pulszky Society established the national Museum of the Year program. An Exhibition of the Year award was created, as well as Visitor-friendly Museum and Family-friendly Museum awards based on online votes of visitors. Prizes that stimulate excellence in educational activities, for example, Benchmark-prizes for education programs or educational publications, are now given annually by the public collections department of the responsible ministry.

The Inspectorate mentioned before was renewed. Its new museum education branch (MEB) organized a one-day conference that brought together sixty

A new fashion: Visitors may visit the "scenic storage" of museums. Here a detail of that is seen in the Open Air Museum, Szentendre.

The newly established, visitor-friendly museum in Gyöngyös. It was the Museum of the Year in 2010.

educators from museums around the country in order to discuss *their* expectations of the newly established Inspectorate. The MEB subsequently developed a 20-page questionnaire given to museum professionals that left room for self-evaluation. The MEB also organized annual conferences that brought together museum educators and schoolteachers in ever-increasing numbers.

The MEB also participated in the organization and professional performance of outstanding countrywide events. For example, Museum Mayday is a weekend event when over 100 museums appear in tents in downtown Budapest's Museum Garden and offer educational and entertaining programs. It is a very popular museum event. The Museums' Autumn Festival is a weeks-long series of loose-fitting programs. In 2011, one hundred and seventy museums offered special programs in October-November, and centralized PR of the events provided great publicity. This event is meant to inform teachers about the new offerings of the museums in the school year.

Long Night of Museums has suddenly become the most popular of these programs. On the Saturday nearest to Midsummer Night, most museums stay open until midnight or beyond, and offer special programs like lectures, shows, theater, music, and dance. This attracts, beyond regular museum-goers, a great and wide audience. Visitors seem to behave differently this evening, the program being more social than academic. For some museums this is by far the most visited event in the year. In Budapest, a change in the nightlife of the city is palpable on these occasions; the streets are busier as visitors try to reach and enjoy several museums using passes. Besides attracting visitors, these events provide opportunities for museum professionals to share experiences, learn from each other, and work towards improving the public performance of Hungarian museums.

Arts and crafts in the Museum Mayday, 2012. The text of the poster tells: I LOVE YOU MÚZEUM.

New Social Responsibilities in Museums

Over the last few decades, some museums in Hungary have broadened the scope of their activities beyond traditional museum topics and studies. Many now deal with issues important for society.

For example, existing buildings have been transformed into memorial museums. The most famous of these is the House of Terror Museum, which was established in a building that formally served as the headquarters for the Nazi occupiers of World War II and the secret police of the Communist era. Opened in 2002, the House of Terror is a monument to the memory of those held captive, tortured, and killed in this building (by Nazis, and soon after by Communists). "The museum, while presenting the horrors in a tangible way, also intends to make people understand that the sacrifice for freedom was not in vain." This mission is also accomplished through changing, temporary exhibitions on related issues, for example the exhibition *Hungarian Tragedy, Southland, 1944–1945* (on two simultaneous holocausts in a historical part of Hungary).

Established in a reconstructed synagogue, the Holocaust Memorial Center introduces the history of the Jewish and Roma holocaust through real familial and personal fates. A core mission is to develop tolerance in the community by putting the Holocaust in a wider social context. Their traveling exhibition, *Auschwitz Album — About Them, for Us, without Them*, is on its way to being shown in 28 locations in Hungary and in surrounding towns with many Hungarian minorities or (local) majorities.

The building of the Holocaust Memorial Center and Museum, in Budapest.

A third example of an institution housed in a repurposed building is Memorial Point in the town Hódmezővásárhely. This museum was created in a 300-year old, fully modernized building, and bases its exhibits on the town's Communist past. (Ironically enough, the museum is situated on Andrássy Street, which during the Communist era was called Stalin Street.)

Another serious social issue, the environmental crisis, is now highlighted by a few natural history museums. The Móra Ferenc Múzeum in Szeged opened the first in the 1980s with the title *We Have Only One Earth*. In 1996, the Hungarian Natural History Museum (HNHM), which had moved into an old military academy a few years before, opened a new visitor space with an environmental education exhibition called *Man and Nature in Hungary*. This space now houses an exhibit on biodiversity. The co-operation of HNHM with the Hungarian Society for Environmental Education has brought new topics and new methods into museum education.

Educate the Educators

Formal training of museum educators, an important condition of good performance and development that was started in the 1970s, was interrupted for two decades. In 2000, a law was passed that mandated vocational training of museum staff and teachers alike (120 hours in a seven-year period for most employees).[13] Museum education as a subject entered the programs of eight universities. The largest training, a two-year Museum Education professional postgraduate course, taught mostly by museum professionals in museum spaces, is run by ELTE University. The program enrolls 15 to 25 participants a year, from schools and museums alike.

A tremendous change came in 2009 with the establishment of MOKK (Education and Training Centre of Museums) as a branch of the Hungarian Open Air Museum. With a substantial national grant, a three-year project has been started to improve the communication and community oriented functions of museums, and their relationship with school education. The Inspectorate has helped to clarify new social needs, to discover cultural market forces, and to consider academic development, as well as to recognize the significance of up-to-date communication and social dialogue. Ten different courses were developed on topics related to museum management, exhibition making, publications, programs, educational issues in museums, and networking and co-operation with schools. Courses are free of charge, and they take place one to two times a year. There have been 470 participants since 2009, which is about one-fifth of all graduate museum workers in Hungary. The Centre has published books and course materials, and has developed free e-learning courses, with free downloads for registered users of the web site. The centre also established a regional network of advisors who organize conferences and other professional events to support local colleagues.

In 2011, ELTE University started a new Science Communication Masters program (MSc) with museum interpretation as one of the majors.[14] It is the first program of its kind in Eastern Europe. With the cooperation of museums, a course book, *Museum Learning*, was also published by an international panel of authors that included George Hein and David Anderson.

There are also informal and in-service methods of professional training. Since 2004, Hungary has been a member of the European Union, and an exhausting but fruitful way of improvement has been participation in EU-funded multinational projects. The results are slowly becoming visible. For example, the School and Museum Education Cooperation (SMEC) initiative resulted in a one-week internship training housed by the Deutsches Museum in Munich, Germany.[15] Another recent project, Natural Europe, aimed at supporting high quality visits to museums by providing educational pathways, was developed in co-operation with teachers.[16] This project developed didactic materials and some e-learning contents which are available for all who want to improve, including museum educators.

All these developments have helped museum educators and museums improve their work and results according to the international trend towards visitor orientation, but they are possibly too late or too slow to protect museums in the recent situation.

Present Tensions and Challenges

Hungary inherited a rich, tangible cultural heritage in the form of a large museum system. Museum professionals and government officials alike made serious efforts in the last decades to maintain the museums and provide access to the wealth preserved there. The results of these strategic activities are visible in rising attendance between 2004 and 2006, but then the global and national economic crisis took hold. Municipal support of museums fell by 20 to 30% in most counties in 2010–2011. In Hungary, as of January 2012, county museum networks have become state property, and government support for national museums has fallen by 20%. Further cutbacks are forecasted for the coming years. Museums in Hungary are at a crossroads, and not for the first time.

Farewell Party in the recently refurbished Foundry Museum. The occasion: Most of the staff were laid off due to downsizing in 2012.

Hungary is in a politically, economically, and socially sensitive, fluid period. Most museums change slowly, as they have a historical existence and are meant to preserve cultural goods for eternity. This is in itself a handicap in a time of quick globalization and the breakthrough of the virtual world. People are less interested in the real world (including our highly valued, authentic objects of national cultural heritage) and visitors demand virtual, interactive tools in museum spaces. Curators want to exhibit scientific ideas; the public wants to enjoy the visit. It is an open question how Hungarian museums will answer these and other challenges.

These years may mean a sort of cataclysm for Hungarian museums and museum education. It is up to us to save our museums. This is not just a financial issue, or a task only for managers and financial and marketing experts. It is also a task for educators. A similarly important task is to keep society interested in museums, to increase the wish and intention of our communities — as well as the commitment of decision makers — to enjoy, use, and maintain museum resources. To accomplish this task, it is necessary to achieve more cohesion and unity among museums and museum educators in order to heal the "Hungarian patient."

Acknowledgments

The author is much indebted to the editors for their care and attention in improving the manuscript.

Notes

1. This paper is partly based on previous analyses by the author and on other Hungarian language publications which are not cited due to lack of space.
2. In Hungary, museums were and are under strong legal control. The 1927 Museum Law decreed that the cultural heritage of Hungary was the property of the country, the government had a right to control its preservation, and that registration of the collection items was compulsory.
3. We may rightfully find these goals matching many recent museum mission statements, for example, "to provide entertaining learning possibilities for the widest possible audience." The difference, of course, is the political, ideological content.
4. This museum later showed self-critical attitudes and evolved into a museum of contemporary history.
5. An inspector was similar to a museum advisor, who was not invited (contracted) by the museum, but sent by the museum authority. This control was, at least in the field of natural history, not political. However, the staff members who served as inspectors were disinterested or untrained in communication or education issues.
6. The International Council of Museums is the worldwide organisation of museums based on individual and institutional memberships. It has national committees as well as academic committees, and helps the existence and development of museums by networking, conferences, publications, and by developing standards for them.
7. Characteristic to the spirit of the age is that the Curator's Council of HNHM felt it necessary to announce in a resolution that they support the preservation, or even possible growth of the education activities and staff of the museum.
8. In 2009, nineteen such persons published their "stories" in a separate book that told of the tricks and solutions used during periods of financial distress. These helped them maintain interest in their museum.
9. This refers to some very important achievements: the end of party power, freely elected Parliament and local municipalities, market economy, free exchange of currency accompanied with arbitrary visits of foreign countries, free practice of one's religion, freedom of speech, formation of civic organisations.
10. Let me mention a personal experience from that time. HNHM was offered a 6-week exchange program by AAM in 1991. Ms. Pam Tooley came to Budapest from the Heard Natural Science Museum (McKinney, Texas), and studied Hungarian museum education in various institutions. In exchange I spent my time in McKinney and learned that the small Heard Museum had the same attendance as my big, national museum. I also participated in the AAM Annual meeting. Since the Tooley and Gerron family offered me free accommodation (together with their invaluable friendship), I could prolong my stay and visit the natural history museums in New York and Washington. I came back with a new understanding of the social functions and tasks of museums, and the experience gave me the impetus to apply for the educational deputy position in my museum.
11. See www.muzeumokmindenkinek.hu.
12. See www.museum.hu/services/mk/files/mk_2009_1.pdf, or, the whole study in English: http://www.museum.hu/services/mk/mk.php?IDMK=1730.
13. At the moment the government support for this process is suspended, due to the financial situation of the state.

14. See www.edutech.elte.hu.
15. See www.museoscienza.org/smec.
16. See www.natural-europe.eu.

About the Author

Tamás Vásárhelyi, PhD in zoology, was curator, and deputy director (responsibility: education, exhibitions, and marketing) of the Hungarian Natural History Museum. He has been active in various governmental bodies and civic organizations (museums, biology, environmental education). An active writer in these fields, he has published several books, museums education booklets, and over 250 scientific and popular papers.

Art Museum Education in Transition

Moderna galerija in Slovenia

Adela Železnik

Abstract   This essay examines the educational practices at the Moderna galerija, a national museum of modern and contemporary art in Ljubljana, Slovenia, in the last twenty years. Its aim is to reflect on the museum education in relation to broader historical context, of the former Yugoslavia (the country Slovenia was a part of until 1991) and discuss how social, political, and economic changes affected art museum education today. A special emphasis is given to the art museum's educational practices in the 1970s, which embodied the socialist doctrine of "education to the people." After the breakup of Yugoslavia, the development of the profession depended on the individual states. The author briefly mentions two museums in the former state where educational practices present case studies of good practice. The main part of the essay concentrates on selected case studies carried out at the Moderna galerija. With the prospects of overcoming the present difficult economical situation, the author hopes that museum educators in the territories of the former Yugoslavia will again find the way to collaborate, appreciate what was worth keeping in the common legacy, and join forces to critically respond to the rising commercialization and popularization representing a threat to all new states in transition.

The Historical Background of Museum Education in a Socialist Country

Moderna galerija was founded in 1948 as a museum of modern and contemporary art. It was among the first modern and contemporary art museums in Yugoslavia and the new museum building was designed in the 1930s by one of the most prominent Slovenian architects of the twentieth century, Edvard

Journal of Museum Education, Volume 37, Number 3, Fall 2012, pp. 31–42.

Ravnikar. Other major national museums of contemporary art were established later: Galerija suvremene umjetnosti/Gallery of Contemporary Art, Zagreb, in 1951; Muzej savremene umetnosti/Museum of Contemporary Art, Belgrade, in 1965; and Muzej na sovremenata umetnost/Museum of Contemporary Art, Skopje, in 1964 (to host the collection donated to the city after the catastrophic earthquake in 1963).

In Yugoslavia all museum activities were very much attuned to the socialist doctrine of self management which proclaimed that art belongs to everyone.[1] Education was therefore one of the central issues in the socialist art museum mission statements, although it never reached the status it had, for instance, in the United States or in the Soviet Union.[2] In one of his speeches at the exhibition opening at the Moderna galerija in 1973, Stane Dolanc, the state secretary of the Executive committee of the Communist Party of Yugoslavia stressed that "art should not be discussed in the 'cultural ghettos' (i.e., museums), where only artists and professional public communicate, but among workers where art gets its real confirmation and meaning."[3] Education was therefore part of the state cultural policy and the educators were supposed to put into practice what the politicians were propagating. Job positions of "curators for education" were mostly established in the late 1960s and early 1970s. The task of these educators was to make bridges between museums and factories (sometimes literally to bring art to the factory workers), to organize educational exhibitions, and to provide visiting school groups with information and guidance. The curators for education were also in charge of public relations — they were supposed to communicate with the audience through newsletters, information sheets, and educational materials, and through the media and the press.

There were also exceptions: Curators for education were able to do their duty in a more advanced way, practicing educational activities similar to what museums are doing today. Some of the best examples of socially oriented educational practices in the former Yugoslavia took place at the Centre for Visual Culture at the Museum of Contemporary Art Belgrade (MoCAB), which was established in 1974 out of the museum's pedagogical department. The main aim of the centre was "education through art" and its activities comprised a series of public seminars and lectures, held both inside the museum and also in cooperation with schools, faculties, and factories, with the goal to reach the broadest public.[4] The programming activities at the centre can be described as early examples of a social approach to the mediation of contemporary art; its curators held guided tours for schoolchildren on Saturdays, which was a rarity at that time; it offered a very popular series of public lectures, Approach to Contemporary Art, for young audiences, and conducted programs for various audiences. The centre developed an exhibition called *Demonstration of Materials in Contemporary Visual Arts* in factories that dealt with mechanics, civil engineering, and the pharmaceutical industry, with the aim to show works of art made from materials very familiar to factory workers. The intention was to make contemporary art more accessible and less abstract and hermetic to them.[5]

Already in the 1970s, the centre was very active in educating the public on new media through presentation of films, discussions and examination of film and video art, as well as presentations of the artists.[6] These activities were revolutionary in comparison to the more conventional programs at the Museum of Contemporary Art which was, at that time, dealing mostly with abstract art.[7]

It would be interesting to know if and how the activities of the Centre for Visual Culture at the Museum of Contemporary Art Belgrade (MoCAB) influenced the institutional educational practices in other parts of Yugoslavia; in Slovenia those activities were completely unknown until recently. Research on the potential collaborations of the curators for education in Yugoslavia will also be needed, complementing the already well-known facts that museums in Yugoslavia did exchange artworks from their collections, and organized touring exhibitions around the country. These networks seem to have been forgotten after the traumatic breakup of the common country, along with the brotherhood and the unity of the socialist time.

Art Museum Education After the Breakup of Yugoslavia

The collapse of the former Yugoslavia that began in 1991 with Slovenian independence, followed by the brutal war that severely affected former republics (now independent countries) along with transition from socialist to capitalist system, left museums with financial and economic problems, and some state art museums remain closed today. Those that are still operating are facing the crisis, forced to concentrate on commercial programs rather than participatory and social ones.

In the late 1990s, after the war, art museums in the former Yugoslavia, and in the Balkans as a whole, were very much affected by the political as well as the economic situation, including a destroyed country on the one side, and symptoms of the "predatory capitalism" typical of societies in transition, on the other. The era of relatively well-supported cultural activities in the 1970s was gone, leaving behind reduced budgets and disillusioned staff.

For instance, in the former Centre for Visual Culture at the Museum of Contemporary Art Belgrade, where four curators used to be employed in the 1970s, only one curator remained in the 1990s. In 2006, the Museum of Contemporary Art Belgrade closed for renovation and has not reopened yet.

The Croatia Museum of Contemporary Art in Zagreb operated in different locations from the time it was founded until 2010, when a new museum building was constructed in the residential area of Zagreb, close to one of the biggest shopping malls in the city. As a result of the ambitions of the state and city authorities, the museum now houses a comprehensive display of the national collection of contemporary art, but faces severe difficulties in maintaining the building. One of the major tasks of its educational department is therefore to attract as much audience as possible, but the department is staffed by only a single curator.

Museum Education in Transition

The educational role of the Moderna galerija was defined in its founding act and the first curator for education was appointed in 1965. Her duties were similar to her colleagues — she was responsible for giving lectures about modern and contemporary art to schoolchildren and others groups, and sometimes she organized outreach programs and didactic exhibitions.[8]

The next curator for education at the Moderna galerija in the 1980s had to divide his work between developing exhibitions and guiding tours, which eventually led to a considerable stagnation in museum education — and the educational programs deteriorated to random interactions with schools.

The early 1990s marked a new phase in museum education. With Slovenia's independence in 1991, Moderna galerija became the principal national institution of modern and contemporary art, and an increasingly active link between the local and the international art world. The new educational programs had to take into consideration new methods and approaches in the art museum education.[9] They were focusing not only on collaboration with schools and professional organizations, but also on targeting individuals in their free time. The first task was to attract young audiences to the museum as well as individual visitors and families. Therefore the museum started to organize a series of Saturday morning workshops. The aim was to familiarize children with modern and contemporary art. The workshops were organized in conjunction with current exhibitions and used the "learning-by-doing" method to interpret the exhibited art works. In 1998, on the occasion of the celebration of Moderna galerija's fiftieth anniversary, the Friends of Moderna galerija Club was founded, while the creative Saturdays came under the formal auspices of the "Minimalists' Club." Children who became members of the club would receive regular invitations to the workshops and have additional membership benefits such as a Christmas party, exhibition of their works at the end of the term, etc. A minimum financial contribution from the parents ensured the continuity of the program. The club did not aim to form future artists, but to teach future museum visitors to be open-minded, inquisitive, creative, and tolerant of what is new and, at first sight, perhaps incomprehensible. In conceiving the program the objectives were to offer an interactive approach to the experiencing exhibition, a creative approach to materials, and use of new media (digital cameras and camcorders for making short films or clips).[10]

In addition to the club's extensive activities in the form of workshops,[11] the museum carried out some bigger, interactive projects in collaboration with artists. The aims of these projects were not to mediate and interpret art works like the previous activities, but rather to comment on the contents of the exhibition and its social or political message. The first project in this series was *My Beautiful Home*, conceived in 1994 to accompany the exhibition *House in Time*.[12] Its idea was to explain the notion of migration in ways that children would understand. It began with a public appeal to children to bring their toys to the Moderna galerija to be given to the children in Bosnia and Herzegovina. When the toys (and also some other objects children wanted to donate) were assembled in the museum, the artists Jože Barši and Tadej Pogačar set up an exhibition, consisting of two installations.[13] The children who had brought their toys or objects had the opportunity of encountering the toys again upon their visit to the exhibition (it was on view for two weeks). They were also invited to the final party, after which the donated toys were packed away in boxes and sent to Bosnia and Herzegovina via the Red Cross. The educational aims of this project were to get children acquainted with the museum and contemporary art such as installation art, but no less important was to encourage solidarity with children in war.

Another educational project, *All But Appearance*, was conceived in 2000 and had no connections to the exhibitions. In collaboration with artists and group of scientists the curators for education made a "Blind Library," a sort of interactive installation with the aim to include the blind people as guides. The objective of this project was to overturn the concept of the modern(ist) museum, where sight is the predominant (if not the only) sense for experiencing artworks, and to encourage visitors to use all senses *except sight* in the museum of modern art. The project was realized with the help of a group of scientists and four artists who were particularly interested in new technologies. After a few months of intensive discussions, the group of twelve people decided to make the "Blind Library," a completely dark room with bookshelves filled with books. Most of them were fixed to the shelves, but some were movable. Those were equipped for making different sounds when being taken off the shelf. According to the sound, the visitor was supposed to guess the content of the book. Visitors had no guidance except a plan of the library in the "waiting room" and the list of books the library contained. During the working process we realized we would need the help of blind people, so we contacted the local Society of the Blind, which gave us some advice and technical facilities (for example, the invitation cards were printed in Braille). Also, two members of the Society volunteered as guides. It was their idea to welcome every visitor, introduce themselves, and say a few words about the project. Then they would lead the visitors to the dark room and stay with them until they finished the visit. A special value of this project was the interaction between the blind, usually underprivileged in everyday life, and visitors in a reverse situation — now they were becoming totally dependent on the blind guides.

In the late 1990s Moderna galerija's exhibition policy focused on the issues related to its historical context of Central and Eastern Europe. The result of this was the Moderna galerija's international collection Arteast 2000+, established in 2000. This pioneering collection of Eastern European post-war avant-garde works dating from the 1960s to the present was displayed in 2000 for the first time, but after that the artworks remained in crates because of the lack of space for a permanent display. In order to overcome the problem with the space, the works were included in temporary exhibitions, called the Arteast exhibitions, dealing with the issues related to the collection, and some of them had also educational projects.[14]

The closing of the Moderna galerija for renovation in 2007 caused a considerable break in its educational activities. Almost at the same time, Moderna galerija became involved in the Radical Education (RE) project.[15] This project started from "a social question, a gap or demand that convenes people around an issue." The issue was radical pedagogy, the concept of a Brazilian pedagogue, Paulo Freire,[16] but also a desire to react to the demands that were more related to the field of politics than art. The aim was to incite social and political changes. One of the members of the Radical Education Collective was also Moderna galerija's curator for education, so the project affected also the Moderna galerija's "institutional" education. Referring to the writings of Paulo Freire and some other critical writers and philosophers (Henry Giroux, Ivan Illich, and especially Jacques Rancière),[17] Moderna galerija switched its attention to collaborative or cooperative learning, based on non-hierarchical, non-institutional connections, with art being only one of the activities involved.

From this period there are two projects, both connected to the Radical Education project and realized in frames of the exhibition *Museum in the Streets* in 2008.[18] One was called *The School on the River*, and was initiated by an activist, Gašper Kralj; the other, *You and the City*, was a project by a Dutch artist Jeanne van Heeswijk. Both projects were related to the situation after the breakup of Yugoslavia — *The School on the River* dealing with the problematic aspects of the official school curricula that do not take into consideration the cultural background of the students and their parents coming from Bosnia and other parts of the previously common country, and *You and the City* with the notion of young women's identity in a society in transition. In both cases Moderna galerija collaborated with the elementary school Livada, located on the outskirts of un-regulated area in the south of Ljubljana, called Rakova Jelša, mostly populated by the migrant workers from Bosnia.

The School on the River, conceived by the activist Gašper Kralj, also had a political agenda. With this project he wanted to call for, and potentially change, social relations propagated by the education system. His idea was to bring a group of school children on a raft down the Ljubljanica river from the Rakova Jelša district through the city center to the Rog Social Center where various activities would take place such as graffiti, music and video workshops for children, and informal debates for adults, including teachers, activists and parents. This

School on the River, Workshop at the Social Center Rog , a courtyard of an abandoned bicycle factory. Photo: Dejan Habicht, © Moderna galerija, Ljubljana

Main characters of the *You and the City* project performance in the city center. Photo: Dejan Habicht, © Moderna galerija, Ljubljana

project was conceived to represent an act of protest on the one hand, and a possibility of starting a debate on the other; and it was supposed to conclude with a barbecue party for all. If the activist's goal was primarily the act itself, the museum's concern, was primarily what to do with the kids on the boat, how to make them aware of what they were doing, i.e., how to make this a valuable learning experience and engage them in the more structured activities, which were to take place in the courtyard. In the end the museum educator suggested the activities for the boat — the children mapped and observed what they saw on the river. The museum invited another artist to teach the participating children how to use cameras and document the boat trip.

The project title *You and the City*, referring to the then very popular TV series, *Sex and the City*, was a participatory art project with no special political agenda. The artist's idea was to "find a revolutionary spirit among the young women," and to encourage teenage girls to write about their views on life, love, career, but also to critically reflect on the society. The project consisted of a series of workshops, and it included a public debate on national TV at the end. Two of the project participants were from the already mentioned Livada elementary school,[19] others were students from another Ljubljana grammar school that was invited to participate by the project educator. One of interesting outcomes of *You and the City* was the realization how the neo-liberal ideology of the country in transition affected young people — they had no desire to change the world, their only wish was to be rich, good-looking, successful, and eventually happy.

After the Moderna galerija re-opened in 2009, it has returned to the more institutional forms of gallery education, [20] but continued to collaborate with the Livada elementary school.[21]

In 2010, when Moderna galerija organized an exhibition on Yugoslavian experimental film, the curator for education took the opportunity to "turn back to the roots," to the historical "case studies of good practice," where elements of critical pedagogy can be found. This project was related to film education, which was extremely well-developed in the 1970s and 1980s in the former Yugoslavia even though it was never practiced in the museums. (Only the initiatives of the Centre for Visual Culture in Belgrade used some of its methods.) There were some genuine elements of comradeship in the profession: film directors and educators were closely collaborating; film festivals were organized all over the country to exchange experiences; educators on film education from all parts of Yugoslavia were learning from each other.[22]

The latest turning point in the Moderna galerija's activities was the opening of the new unit of the Moderna galerija — the Museum of Contemporary Art Metelkova — in November 2011.[23] The building used to be a Yugoslav army barracks, now being renovated and forming part of the new museums quarter at the Metelkova district. The concept of the new museum is an antithesis of the modernist one, with large emphasis given to the participation of visitors. A considerable part of the museum's ground floor is therefore designed for the active use of the visitors. In cooperation with the Slovene artist, Apolonija Šuštaršič, one of the spaces is meant to introduce the visitors various local, regional, and broader international networks in which Moderna galerija collaborates and offer friendly and welcoming atmosphere with comfortable chairs and coffee. On the ground floor there is also a conference room and a studio, mostly used for lectures and workshops.

Considering the new facilities, the museum education gained more space and recognition but, considering the staffing, the situation remained more or less the same as in the 1970s. Even though in this "golden era" education seemed to have an important role in "cultural empowerment of the working people," there was never more than one person employed for this task. After forty years, the situation is the same, or worse. The Moderna galerija has two museum buildings, but still only one person responsible for education, which is growing more and more extensive. In the 21st century, after the often quoted "educational turn"[24] new questions appeared for the education practitioners: how can knowledge be exchanged without being patronizing, how can knowledge of all participants be included, and especially how can our visitors be encouraged to take part in this co-production of knowledge?

Conclusion

In the socialist period, due to self-management, some of the examples of educational activities that took place in the former Yugoslavian art museums can now be seen as having emancipatory potential, as critical pedagogy demands of education today.[25] Artists were equal to workers. If workers did not come to the museum and galleries to experience art, artists and museum workers would come to the factories; museum workers would organize a didactic exhibition and artists would co-produce their works in situ.[26] Today, when the economical crisis affected all layers of public life, arts and culture are no longer recognized as a value but more as an unwanted cost and burden to the society. Moreover, the new state authorities all over the territory of the former Yugoslavia demand that the cultural sector to be held accountable in the same ways as the business sector. The success of a museum is measured by the number of visitors, and museums and art galleries all over the territory are closing due to the lack of financial support.

Art museum education curators in the previously mentioned museums in former Yugoslavia know each other, but do not collaborate. At this time of crisis, in 2012 we need to find new ways of solidarity and collaboration. So that museum education will be again the profession to prove that art and culture must be "the essential need and an intrinsic right of every individual."

Notes

1. In the socialist system art was treated as one of the "sources of the power and stability of the masses." The socialist ideologists would call its cultural policy a plurality of choices "a hundred flowers blooming in the field." Workers were supposed to have an active part in culture, not only as its consumers but rather as its creators, self-managing people who experience culture as their essential need as well as their intrinsic right.
2. Breda Misja, the first curator of education at the Moderna galerija, made a comparison with the United States, the Soviet Union, and the Democratic Republic of Germany. See Breda Misja, Pedagoško delo v galerijskih ustanovah/Pedagogical Work in the Galleries, (Argo, 1973, 1, XII/No. 1–2), 20–27.
3. Čestitke, obračuni in načrti. 60 let Moderne galerije/Congratulations, Summations, and Plans — 60 Years of the Moderna galerija, (documentary exhibition catalogue (in Slovenian only), 2008), 15.
4. Zoran Erić and Una Popović, "Centre for visual culture at MoCAB" in Communication Networks, exhibition catalogue (Ljubljana: Mestna galerija, March 2010), 31.
5. Ibid., 32–34.

6. This was one of the courses led by Jasna Tijardović, curator at the Centre from 1975 to 1989. Together with her husband, film director Zoran Popović, Jasna Tijardović, was teaching Yugoslav contemporary art in the USA.

7. Jasna Tijardović wrote about a new approach towards the prevailing modernist art at the Museum of Contemporary Art while working at the Centre. "I made a number of exhibitions that were related to my 'conceptual' and other backgrounds finding a balance between the interests of the museum and my own in order to mediate the new artistic productions." See also: http:/radical.temp.si/.

8. Didactic exhibitions were not organized very often due to the notorious lack of funds and they did not include works from the collection, but mostly prints borrowed from the artists.

9. In 1993, the third regularly employed curator for education in Moderna galerija's history started conceiving education programs from the beginning.

10. More about the club's activities on www.mg-lj.si/node /459.

11. There was no special space for the workshops so they usually took place either in the exhibition rooms or outside the museum (in the summer).

12. The international exhibition took place at the time of war in Bosnia and many artworks related to the issue of migration (e.g., Christian Boltanski).

13. More about the project see Adela Železnik, "My Beautiful Home," M'ARS, Magazine of the Modern Art Ljubljana, (Year VII, 1995, No. 3–4), 62–65.

14. For example the exhibition Interrupted Histories, 2006, was accompanied by an educational project, Do we know each other?

15. The project was initiated by the Moderna galerija exhibition curator and some activists, its activities were partly carried out in frames of the museum's program even though the project remained independent. The basic idea of the Radical Education project was to translate radical pedagogy into the sphere of cultural, non-material production, with education being conceived not merely as a model/tool but also as a field of political participation. Cf. http://temp.radical.si.

16. Especially his seminal work Pedagogy of the Oppressed (New York, London: Continuum, 2005).

17. This is to refer to Rancière's seminal book, The Ignorant Schoolmaster. See Jacques Rancière: The Ignorant Schoolmaster: Five Lessons in Intellectual Emancipation (Palo Alto: Stanford University Press, 1991).

18. http://www.mg-lj.si/node/189 (accessed on April 20, 2012).

19. Almina came with her family from Bosnia some months ago and did not speak Slovenian; the other, Tugs, who spoke Slovenian and English well, was from a migrant family from Mongolia and temporarily lived in the state migrant centre close to the Rakova Jelša district.

20. Cf.://www.mg-lj.si/node/28; (only partly in English).

21. Just a month after the School on the River, a Brazilian collective, Contra File, who had been invited to participate in the Encounter on Radical Education, led a workshop where students were local guides to their neighborhood. Two years ago a workshop was organized in their school, led by two curators of the exhibition entitled Home, one them an architect, Anja Planišček, continued to work with students. She lent them cameras to take photographs in their homes, and last February they were making books in the museum.

22. The museum organized a round table with the pioneers of film education in Slovenia, other events and talks included film directors from Serbia, Croatia, Bosnia and Herzegovina.

23. Another of Moderna galerija's founding acts in 2004 included two units, a museum of modern art and a museum of contemporary art, but this division of work was realized only in 2011 when the new building was finished.

24. Cf. Irit Rogoff, "Turning," www.e-flux.com/journal/view/18 and Nora Sternfeld, "Unglamorous Tasks: What Can Education Learn from its Political Traditions?" www.e-flux.com/journal/view/125.

25. For example, the activities of the Centre for Visual Culture at the Museum of Contemporary Art Belgrade.
26. "Forma viva" was a sort of artist-in-residence program, where artists were temporarily working in the factory and in exchange for the materials, they left their works to the factory and its workers.

About the Author

Adela Železnik graduated in art history and English, MA in art history from the University of Ljubljana, Slovenia. She was a visiting student at the University of London/ Goldsmiths College, London, in 1992–1993. Since 1993, she has worked at the Moderna galerija as a curator for education and public programs, located in the Museum of Contemporary Art Metelkova (MSUM) since 2011.

The *1+1:Life & Love* Simultaneous Exhibition

Cross-border Collaboration in the Western Balkans

Diana Walters

Abstract   This article describes and analyzes a cross-border, "simultaneous exhibition" collaborative project in six post-conflict western Balkan countries. Through a process of collaboration, active learning, and audience development, professional and personal trust developed among eleven museums. Previously identified barriers were overcome and expectations of the original project were surpassed leading to a shared joint-platform, visible collaboration, and an international profile. The case study provides a model for museum collaboration and trust-building among different organisations.

The Western Balkan Region

The break-up of the former Yugoslavia in the latter part of the twentieth century was followed by years of political conflict, war, ethnic cleansing, and trauma. As new nations were formed, the region fragmented with hostile and aggressive proclamations of identity, territory, and symbolism. The human toll of these ongoing troubles is difficult to grasp. According to political scientist Susan Woodward, approximately 200,000 fled Croatia, creating the largest refugee crisis in Europe since 1945.[1] In Bosnia-Herzegovina, more than 70,000 died in the first two years of the war and nearly half the population became refugees "or were displaced to other parts of the republic, expelled from their homes — probably never to return — by fear, war, or nationalist extremists aiming to rid their town or village of people whose ethnicity was different. Among its repercussions was the largest global dispersement of children since World War II."[2] Other crises in

Journal of Museum Education, Volume 37, Number 3, Fall 2012, pp. 43–56.

the region continued for several years; the NATO bombing of Serbia, the war in Kosovo, and ethnic tension in Macedonia have all left their scars in this troubled and unsettled area of South Eastern Europe.

Heritage and Conflict

According to Yvonne Whelan, a cultural and historical geographer, heritage is a highly politicized process and instances of its impact can be mapped throughout the Balkan crises.[3] As part of ethnic cleansing, landscapes, symbols, buildings, and traditions were systematically erased from whole areas. Religious buildings such as mosques and churches were targeted, but vernacular architecture, language, and festivals were also victims of cultural erasure. In this context, museums become potentially powerful political institutions. They construct and communicate messages about identity, history, culture, and what is valued in society at a given point in time. In the Balkans, most museums are government-funded, meaning that they are to a large extent controlled by the politicians. Directors may be appointed by political parties with a clear mandate to strengthen a particular (narrow) agenda and they may also lack relevant competence, for example in working knowledge of the cultural sector or managing staff.

The Balkan Museum Network

However, it is possible to find examples of cross-border collaboration. This is increasing among NGOs, but for official institutions, post-conflict co-operation is more challenging and several obstacles exist. As well as the obvious political difficulties, for example between Serbia and Kosovo, where the former country does not recognise the legitimacy of the latter, there are layers of practical hindrances such as multiple languages, disputed borders, visa restrictions, customs barriers, and economic and social instability.

These challenges are considerable for museum professionals. Much of the cross-border work that does take place is a direct result of international intervention. Cultural Heritage without Borders (CHwB) is an independent, Swedish-based organisation active in the Balkans since 1995. Predominantly funded through Sida (the Swedish International Development and Co-operation Agency), CHwB "is neutral when it comes to conflicting parties, but not to the rights of all people to their cultural heritage."[4] In 2006, CHwB facilitated a regional museum project with eleven museums from six countries. Six of these were national institutions from Albania, Bosnia-Herzegovina, Kosovo,

Macedonia, Montenegro, and Serbia; two were small historic houses; and three were city or regional museums. Many had already worked with CHwB and all had shown interest in a shared platform. For some museums it was the first contact they had had with each other since the war and they took some political risk in joining. The museum network represented a step into regional cross-border work underpinned by broad principles of museums as potential agents of democracy and social change and a commitment to strengthening professional links, reaching new audiences, and promoting dialogue.

Creative solutions:
The Simultaneous Exhibition Approach

The network organised meetings, seminars and workshops exploring topics such as conservation, education, marketing, leadership, and access. Good working relationships began to develop based on common problems and needs. The idea of a joint exhibition was discussed from the outset, but although the concept of common heritage was accepted, the idea was rejected as being too complicated and politically fraught, with several colleagues expressing open opposition. In 2010 the proposal was discussed again and though reservations still existed there was more solidarity and trust between partners. An internal evaluation revealed a significant shift towards joint projects, with one Serbian director commenting that "it is important to have different heritage researched, presented, and discovered as part of mutual heritage and it is important for the Balkan countries to communicate and understand past and current situations."[5] In a creative problem-solving environment the idea of a simultaneous exhibition was born. The objectives were to expand openness and democracy in museums and to actively challenge negative representations of the Balkans through celebrating the common heritage. It was also agreed to target young people and to produce professional, high quality exhibitions. Thus on March 11, 2011, eleven museums in six western Balkan countries simultaneously opened exhibitions all with the title, *1+1:Life & Love*. The openings were live-streamed and around the world over 5000 people watched or supported them through Facebook and other social media.[6]

The *1+1:Life & Love* simultaneous exhibition can be viewed through various lenses. It was an example of how collaborative working can create trust between people whose recent experiences have been of conflict and division. It was an example of active learning and audience development, whereby new methods, ideas, and approaches were introduced and tested in a broadly constructivist mode. It showed the importance of process and participation in externally driven projects. It also demonstrated the actual and potential role of the wider international museum community as observers and advocates through the adoption of new media. These positions are considered throughout, and also the points at which they intersect.

1+1:Life & Love: The Concept

A working group took on the task of producing a proposal for directors. The group was predominantly younger people, comprised of curators and one educator. There was unanimous agreement that the theme should not relate to recent history of the region and to actively avoid the potential pitfalls of contested history and politics. Sociologist Barbara Misztal refers to the balancing between the "duty to remember" and "the duty to forget" in the face of past traumas, but this was more a case of conscious avoidance.[7] The universality of "life and love" appealed to all and in discussions one young archaeologist from Sarajevo summed up the feeling as "we shall never forget, but we cannot stay forever on the battlefield."

The prefix "*1+1*" requires explanation. The risks involved in sharing a public platform, particularly for colleagues from Serbia and Kosovo meant that at any point up to the openings, participants might pull out. Equally, there was determination to show that the project was a *joint* venture and that *somehow* the museums would link together. An Albanian museum director worked on the idea of hidden symbols and developed the *1+1* logo. *1+1* represented the oneness of "life and love," but also symbolized relationships and the 11 museums in the group. The animation of the numbers represented the aspiration that the project

The 1+1 Logo, from a design by Fatmir Juka.

would foster a spirit of co-operation and mutuality by "reaching for the stars." The logo was powerful and popular, with many museums developing their own style and identity.

Participatory Project Management: Creative Chaos

The whole project was executed in under two years at minimal cost. At every stage the process was participatory, meaning that all colleagues were encouraged to contribute. In total, over sixty people were involved, with a core group of twenty-two. Participants included directors, curators, educators, administrators, designers, technicians, PR and marketing staff plus volunteers and external partners. Managing the project was a considerable logistical challenge; no common language, different working styles, physical distance, and cautiousness affected progress throughout.

The project started with the task and success criteria, and then developed roles for committed people. This flexible approach meant that a fully functioning stable team was never achieved, as different institutions applied different criteria to the selection of participants. Two organizational cultures collided. The external facilitators assumed that the process of creating stable teams led by project managers would be straightforward and uncontroversial. In fact, few institutions used this approach. An internal evaluation with directors showed that participation in CHwB activities was usually a reward or given in rotation; opportunities for individual staff were not to be at the expense of the existing hierarchy. Elisa Harrocks, a masters student at Gothenburg University and intern for CHwB analyzed other CHwB-driven museum projects and highlighted a basic dilemma between the characteristics of a successful project and the requirements for organizational learning and change, with CHwB motivated more by the latter than the former.[8] In other words, for CHwB (and some directors) the process was more important than the outcome.

Occasionally it proved impossible to find consensus and the external facilitator made decisions. This was done openly and was accepted as pragmatic and necessary and illustrated the importance of sustainability and leadership. The project developed through a series of workshops, bringing the whole team together or with smaller groups of specialists, and individual exhibitions were developed in between times. Progress and challenges were shared and discussed, reinforcing openness and strengthening solidarity. Informal communication developed between partners and strong ties of professional support and friendship blossomed. Nevertheless, the process often felt chaotic and stressful. Internal organizational difficulties, disagreements, change, and disputes were common, making it an ongoing task to keep everyone engaged and moving forward. Leaders and champions emerged and the positive team spirit was absolutely essential to the project. Cecilia Ljungman & June Taboroff, independent evaluators appointed by Sida, found that "interviews reveal that the positive and negative group experience along the way — not least the launching of the simultaneous exhibition — has cemented bonds among this Balkan museum community.[9]

Learning Together: New Audiences and Approaches

A key objective of *1+1:Life & Love* was to engage with young people. Several museums linked their exhibitions with a parallel initiative on access and adopted inclusive approaches, meaning that disabled and non-disabled people worked together in shared spaces. Many of the museums reported increased attendances of young people; in Novi Sad, Serbia, about 20% of the 8,000 visitors were young and in Tirana, Albania, one curator reported that the creation of a child-friendly interactive space in the museum had "transformed us. We now realize that children in Tirana have so little to do and so few places to go, so they have started to come here. We are so happy."

For some museums, working with young people as a target group was new and challenging, and in practice it was executed unevenly, despite several relevant preparatory workshops. Balkan museums are broadly traditional and not appealing to younger people. There are few museum educators and learning is biased more towards the academic and scientific. Audience development is rare and evaluation almost non-existent. What activities there are tend to be focused on younger children and are rarely integrated into formal or informal learning structures. The museums lack both confidence and skills in reaching new audiences, but they are also hampered by a lack of political will. They are not expected to be socially active and consequently their value is low in civil society. However, every museum did involve young people somehow, and for some this was a significant shift in attitude and operation. Engagement ranged from fully integrated projects that created new platforms to one-off art events for friends and family.

Other developments were less successful but had major impact. The decision to use live-streaming to coordinate the openings in virtual space was taken late in the day and did not work well. Several museums had not road-tested the technique, resulting in technological chaos on the opening night. However, the significance of live-streaming cannot be overstated. It took the event to an international audience and Diaspora communities. Thousands logged on and were effectively acting as observers in an ongoing mediation process. This is a role the international museum community should embrace and develop. The joint website was more successful technologically and became a hub of activity before the openings, showing several short videos and promotional material.[10] Support from the Swedish Embassies in the various cities was also a key factor in ensuring widespread press interest. Many of the openings were well supported and highly successful, with some museums reporting their biggest-ever attendances. In Sarajevo, people were standing outside the National Museum, and in Tirana the whole of the main gallery, 300 square meters (3,230 square feet) was full. Within the group, messages of support were sent to each other, prompting one colleague from Serbia to write "I want to say how nice it is to receive invitations and hear the news about the openings on the same date from ten other places....A very good feeling!"

Finding the Common Ground

Another challenge was displaying the "rich and common heritage" across all exhibitions. In practice, commonality was more accidental than planned, and despite several attempts to work with agreed-upon themes, each museum went its own way. However, shared characteristics did emerge. Several museums used visual art and interpreted life and love through classic representations from nature, mythology, and (broadly conventional) relationships. Both of the small historical museums chose traditional costume and textiles. Two national

"*1+1: Life & Love*" at Novi Sad City Museum (photographed by the author).

museums adopted an interdepartmental approach, moving from classification to thematic exhibition construction for the first time. Only in one museum was there evidence of an agenda that was felt to be counter to the peace and reconciliation spirit of *1+1*, and that was a call for repatriation of objects.

Within the group itself, differences of interpretation were not felt to be problematic. This may reflect what Elizabeth Crooke, an expert on museums and communities has identified as "the rituals and characteristics of particular groups [that] become cultural codes, the meanings of which are understood by the members and recognized by others as belonging to a particular community."[11] Despite recent events, the group displayed a high level of cultural regularity, which possibly means that many values, principles, and behaviors were mutually understood and showed deeper levels of homogeneity rooted in centuries of shared history.[12] This may partly explain the relative ease with which a joint catalogue and a common opening panel were eventually produced despite these being viewed with suspicion initially. Both of these were in English, as resources would not stretch to multiple languages and also because lack of a common language proved a major stumbling block. Through them a design identity was developed and the joint working became visible.

Collaboration, Organizational Learning, and Trust

At the outset, the collaborative nature of *1+1: Life & Love* was unfamiliar and sometimes uncomfortable. Professor of social ethics, Herbert Kelman talks about the need for a gradual building of trust as part of a reconciliation process and the risks involved even when there are obvious interests in making peace.[13] He identifies "a basic dilemma: Parties cannot enter into a peace process without some degree of mutual trust, but they cannot build trust without entering a peace-process."[14] Kelman's work is based on formal peace-process negotiations in post-conflict situations, but his findings are transferable to other settings with groups in mediation. He argues that fostering "working trust" is more fruitful than communal relationships, the difference being that the former is based on a sense of serious commitment to mutuality for clear benefits rather than a sense of shifting to accommodate the other's position, which would probably not be sustained.[15] He goes on to say that personal relations do play a role and that over time interpersonal trust and working trust may merge.[16] This was indeed the case with *1+1*.

Five years of workshops and seminars had laid the foundations for working trust, but the joint project process allowed interpersonal trust to develop. This was supported by an independent evaluation of the museum network in late 2011:

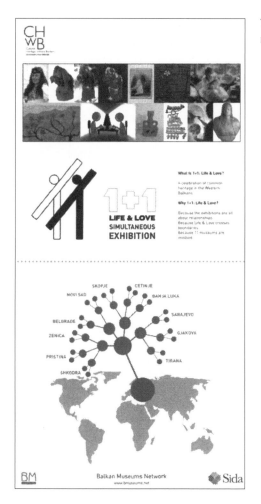

The opening panel displayed in all 11 museums.

From initially reserved, skeptical and even oppositional positions, friendships, camaraderie, and trust have grown among members. This atmosphere now allows for much more active, engaged and open discussions during workshops. Recently, even topics related to the past conflicts in the region have been raised and discussed in an open manner. The fact that museum directors decided to participate in the simultaneous exhibition despite the risk of being fired speaks for the dedication and commitment to the network and what it stands for.[17]

However, Harrocks argued that to achieve a sustained shift of organizational behavior (i.e., to continued participatory or democratic practice), trust needed to be felt across the whole museum and not just be located within one specific group.[18] This is a major challenge for external projects where frequently the aims are *both* to develop relationships between groups who have reason to regard each other with suspicion and inform cultural shifts in practice, and underline the absolute necessity of sustainable interventions as opposed to short-term solutions.

The process of *1+1* is also interesting as an example of organizational learning. The workshops constituting both review and planning created opportunities for "double-loop-learning" and in turn fostered empowerment, responsibility and reflection.[19]

Achieving the Unachievable

At the outset of the project, several barriers to collaboration were identified and many felt genuine concern and fear. However, the project's creative momentum slowly reduced these and fostered infectious positive energy. Late one night, after sharing excellent Balkan food and drink, the idea emerged of organizing a bus tour to visit all of the exhibitions and link people together. The resulting "Peace Bus" visited all eleven partners and travelled from snowy Bosnia-Herzegovina to sunny Montenegro in ten days, crossing seven borders (often with some difficulty and with several sweeteners to appease border guards). Over thirty people joined the tour, for one or more days, including museum partners, family members, a film crew, exhibition contributors, and volunteers. At each museum the group was warmly welcomed and the famous Balkan hospitality shone through. The tour included several small excursions, including a visit to the Decani Monastery in Kosovo.[20] One older Albanian lady reflected that "the main outcome of the bus tour is friendship and especially with Serb women because this relationship is missing. You maybe won't believe how happy I was when the priest at the Decani Monastery greeted the Director of the Pristina museum in Albanian. I said to myself, is it possible to respect each other as human beings? Yes, this can happen if we respect everybody."

When *1+1* is viewed through the lens of interculturalism, a key driving force for international intervention, it is important that the unique characteristics of the Balkans are understood. The economic and social historian Monika Murzyn argued that the area "possessed its own unique features, stemming from the region's geographical location, its peculiar, turbulent history, as well as ethnic and religious diversity."[21] This uniqueness is potentially a rich source of knowledge for the museum and heritage world, where existing literature in this field is biased towards post-colonial perspectives and museums as facilitators of intercultural

The *1+1* Peace Bus (photographed by the author).

dialogue between themselves and communities. The Balkans have a long history of diversity and co-existence with generations of fluidity between borders, ethnicities, and religions, yet it remains under researched as a potential resource for museums elsewhere seeking to engage in intercultural work. There is also a difference in the way that many of these countries are "in transition" compared to other former communist states.[22]

1+1:Life & Love Moves On: The Travelling Exhibition

The success of the simultaneous exhibitions has meant that a joint exhibition will travel from autumn 2012. What was dismissed as impossible is now being created, and the story will, hopefully, reach many people internationally. The travelling exhibition represents a platform for achieving the exhibition cohesion that was lacking from the original eleven shows, with co-operation and unity driving the process rather than being an outcome. The vision statement for the travelling exhibition is "to promote dialogue and diversity and to bridge young people everywhere," and visitors as they enter the show will be greeted by the sentence "(Re)move the boundaries and meet in life and love." The content will be arranged to show the commonality among the exhibitions through themes designed to appeal to younger audiences: journeys in life, spiritual life, earth and life, passion and togetherness. The exhibition design uses the metaphor of a labyrinth reflecting the complexity of the region, the project, and notions of common heritage, themes around which several educational activities are being developed.

Conclusion

The *1+1:Life & Love* simultaneous exhibition project contains important lessons for international development and museum practice. It illustrates a working method of collaboration that circumvents post-conflict divisions across multiple barriers using exhibition and learning based methods. By facilitating working trust, personal trust was able to emerge and problem-solving approaches reduced or eradicated significant barriers to collaboration, leading to a shared platform, increased confidence, and real steps towards reconciliation.

The project has important lessons for external agencies, including museums, that engage in intercultural dialogue. It demonstrated the importance of adopting flexible, participatory approaches when planning projects and interventions and the central importance of shared learning and educational strategies. The project showed the potential of social media and new technology to enable the international museum community to witness peace and reconciliation processes, a crucial role in active social engagement.

Finally, the project showed a side of the Balkans that is almost never reported: the strength of common and shared heritage and the power of individuals and museums to act as agents of social and political change.

Notes

1. Woodward, S., *Balkan Tragedy: Chaos and Dissolution after the Cold War* (Washington, D.C.: The Brookings Institution, 1995).
2. Ibid., 2.
3. Whelan, Y., *Re-inventing Modern Dublin* (Dublin: Dublin University Press, 2003).
4. The phrase is part of the Mission Statement. See www.chwb.org.
5. CHwB Directors Group: Evaluation and Needs analysis, survey, 2 July 2012.
6. Figures showed that around 3500 followed the events on Facebook and that over 2000 people logged on to the Balkan Museums website during live-streaming. Several email conversations also occurred during the lead-up to the openings, and informal messaging through text and "chat" functions.
7. Misztal, B., *Theories of Social Remembering* (Berkshire/Philadelphia: Open University Press/McGraw-Hill House, 2003).
8. Harrocks, E., *Outside In: The Effect of Externally Driven Projects as a Method of Encouraging Organizational Learning in Museums* (Masters Thesis, University of Gothenburg, Sweden, 2010), 42.
9. Ljungman, C. & Taboroff, J., *Evaluation of Cultural Heritage without Borders, 2008–2011* (Indevelop, Stockholm, 2011) 19. http://www.indevelop.se/publications/publication-evaluation-of-cultural-heritage-without-borders-in-the-western-balkans accessed 26 January 2012.
10. See www.bmuseums.net.
11. Crooke, E. "An Exploration of the Connections among Museums, Community and Heritage," in *The Ashgate Research Companion to Heritage and Identity*, ed. B. Graham and P. Howard (Ashgate, 2008), 416.

12. Spencer-Oatey, H. & Franklin, P. *Intercultural Interaction. A Multidisciplinary Approach to Intercultural Communication* (Palgrave MacMillan, 2009), 35.

13. H. Kelman, "Building Trust Among Enemies: The Central Challenge for International Conflict Resolution." *International Journal of Intercultural Relations* 29 (2005): 639–650.

14. Ibid., 639.

15. Ibid., 646.

16. Ibid., 647.

17. Ljungman & Taboroff, *Evaluation of Cultural Heritage without Borders*, 19.

18. Harrocks, Outside In, 64.

19. C. Argyris, "Double Loop Learning in Organizations" in *Harvard Business Review*, 1997.

20. The Decani Monastery is a 14th century masterpiece with world famous Byzantine frescoes. During the recent war it was a place of sanctuary for all local people, regardless of their religion or ethnicity.

21. M. Murzyn, *Heritage Transformation in Central and Eastern Europe*, 315.

22. Cf. J. Dryzek and L. Holmes, *Post-Communist Democratization: Political Discourses across Thirteen Countries* (Cambridge: Cambridge University Press, 2002).

About the Author

Diana Walters is an international museum and heritage consultant and a project manager for Cultural Heritage without Borders. She specializes in access, intercultural dialogue, staff and strategic development, working with many organizations worldwide. Recently her focus has been on supporting museums and heritage agencies in societies experiencing transition to build trust through partnerships and collaboration.

Beyond Borders

Innovating from Conflict to Community in Public Art Engagement in Holon, Israel

Ziva Haller Rubenstein

Abstract   The story of the Center for Digital Art in Holon is a story of innovation in the face of adversity. At key points of escalation in the Middle East
conflict, this small-scale arts center managed to rise above and beyond the
larger and more traditional museums in Israel to create new models for arts
engagement. This article will present the critical junctions at which the Center
for Digital Art managed to radically innovate art education approaches, con-
textualizing their actions within a larger setting of Israel's culture of conflict.
What emerges is a working model for artistic engagement that prioritizes
community-wide dialogue over target-specific impact, offering new working
methodologies for art education professionals to venture beyond the museum
and straight to the public both as contributors in the artistic process and end-
users of the collaborative work.

Introduction

Amid the backdrop of a deep-rooted conflict in the Middle East, where questions
of authority, borders, and belonging strike at the heart of individual and collective identities, are many nondescript cities across Israel where every day life is
layered with its own set of individual and communal struggles. Zooming in on an
urban or community level, these same questions of authority, of borders, and of
belonging take on different expressions, but draw upon the same core issues.
Since the 1990s, the centrally located Israeli city of Holon has been striving to
improve the quality of life among its residents through a citywide renewal

Journal of Museum Education, Volume 37, Number 3, Fall 2012, pp. 57–68.

program that focuses strongly on an artistic and cultural renaissance. But as new museums, public artworks, recreational centers and cultural events began to dot the cityscape, the real change in Holon did not take place in the biggest and splashiest new museum, but rather, through the innovative efforts of a new media art center that engaged the public in and through art.

This article will explore how the Center for Digital Art in Holon innovated new working models for civic engagement and public discourse through art initiatives, demonstrating how their innovation rose in direct response to the intensified culture of conflict in the Middle East. As waves of terror and war washed over the country, specifically during the Second Intifada of 2000-2002 and the Second Lebanon War in 2006, the Center for Digital Art in Holon responded by shifting the focus of their museum activities. Addressing the core issues of the Middle Eastern conflict and positioning them within an artistic discourse abroad, the center recognized that the same questions plagued individuals in their own "backyard." The result is an innovative model for public engagement, one that is predicated on principles of democracy and relies on art education as the starting point, process, and end result.

Holon: Designing a City out of Sand

Named for the sand dunes on which it was built ("hol" in Hebrew means sand), Holon is located in Israel's central region, on the coastal strip south of Tel Aviv. For more than 70 years, the city of Holon has been known for its industry. Today, the city is home to Israel's second largest industrial zone, and numbers a population of close to 190,000 people.[1] After the establishment of the State of Israel in 1948, Holon built a series of concrete, high rise apartment building blocks that further contributed to Holon's drab and gritty image as a city for a "motley collection of residents from the lower socio-economic strata and a stop on the road to the cemetery (located in nearby Bat Yam)."[2] In 1993, newly elected Mayor Moti Sasson vowed to reinvent Holon as a vibrant and thriving city. His sweeping plan included everything from upgrading the transportation infrastructure to improving educational institutions, and from building new, modern neighborhoods to increasing economic opportunities and growth for individuals and businesses. The pride of the city's plan, however, was its focus on culture and art. From the introduction of commissioned sculptures for its public parks to the construction of several massive museums in the city center, Holon has made significant strides in enhancing public spaces with cultural and artistic programs. Its new Design Museum, completed in 2010 and sweeping architectural wonder designed by world renown Israeli-born designer Ron Arad, testifies to the city's intent to both position itself among leading artistic centers in the world and foster a vibrant public cultural life. As explained on the municipality website,

> The [Design Museum] is a major milestone in the journey to put the discussion and exploration of design on the public agenda, and to incorporate design into the fabric of Holon's urban life. Design is expected to be one of Israel's main export industries in the coming years, which is why Holon believes that promoting this field should be a national priority.

Amid these grand gestures for city reform and regrowth, the municipality also focused inward, supporting targeted efforts to improve its weakest and most downtrodden residents, specifically those living in the pocket of despair: The Jesse Cohen neighborhood.

Established in the 1950s, the Jesse Cohen neighborhood was designed to welcome the large influx of immigrants from Europe, the Middle East, and elsewhere. Since then, however, the Jesse Cohen neighborhood has suffered from a long history of crime and poverty, despite targeted renovation and community rehabilitation efforts in the 1970s. To date, Israeli newspapers continue to give voice to complaints by Jesse Cohen residents about the continued neglect and deterioration of the neighborhood. In stark contrast to the clean, new streets and buildings being developed in other parts of the city, the Jesse Cohen neighborhood still suffers from a lack of basic upkeep of public spaces and buildings, irregular garbage collection, and weekly sewage eruptions. And yet, municipal workers are still quoted as claiming that steps have been, and continue to be taken to improve the neighborhood in many ways.[3]

It appeared that the municipality was stuck in a cycle of futility by early 2010; taking specific steps to fix or repair areas of the Jesse Cohen neighborhood did not yield any significant impact in the minds of those who needed that change the most — Jesse Cohen residents. Instead of perpetuating the same mistakes, the municipality decided over two years ago to turn to the Center for Digital Arts, inviting them to initiate and lead public art projects specifically designed to enhance the lives of residents of the Jesse Cohen neighborhood. The pairing was both purposeful and particular; the Center for Digital Arts, having been established in 2001 by the municipality, was already setting itself apart as an innovator in the field of art education by utilizing art as a medium for social empowerment and public discourse among targeted communities.

Setting New Standards

The Center for Digital Art was founded in 2001 with municipal funding and support in an abandoned school building in Holon. Its original mission was to focus on and promote digital art and new media works. But that all changed in 2002 according to Eyal Danon, Director and Chief Curator of the Center for Digital. As the Intifada erupted and terror captured the hearts and minds of citizens across Israel, "[the center] started asking questions regarding the relevance of our activity to the reality outside. . . as these were times of extreme political tension."[4] That moment of introspection proved significant for the center, leading to a dramatic shift in its activities. The center began to focus its exhibitions more specifically on sociopolitical subjects. Palestinian and Arab artists were actively sought out and invited to collaborate and contribute their artwork to exhibitions, and international venues and partnerships were created as a means of looking beyond the gallery walls for increased opportunities for artistic dialogue with the community. Examples from the center's activities from this period include:

- *"Hilchot Shchenim Perek Bet"* ("The Laws of Neighbors, Chapter 2"), 2003, which examined how art is both a mirror of society and can play a role in changing that same society through understanding the role of media filters, specifically unpacking tactics of war, capitalism, and globalization impacts in the media. Artists from international and local nationalities, including Israeli Jewish, Israeli Arab, and Palestinian artists, collaborated on the works produced and selected for the exhibition, working as cooperatives, in groups or couples.[5]

- *"Losing Control,"* 2004, a joint project the Center for Digital Art and NOMAD in Istanbul that aimed at creating a platform for artistic collaborations between Turkish and Israeli artists.[6]

These in-house exhibitions often offered traditional gallery tours and educational programs for local high school students or pre-arranged groups, where within the center's gallery space, individuals were introduced to the larger concepts within the sociopolitical artwork on view and engaged in a discussion about those same issues. But beyond these 'traditional' approaches to museum art education, often completed through one-time gallery tours, was a daring attempt at art engagement that was not being conducted elsewhere in Israel. The exhibition "Losing Control" for example, was on view in Istanbul, Turkey, not in Israel. And its end goal was a process or a sustainable model for interactivity, as stated on its website: "The aim of the project is to create a platform for a meeting between Turkish and Israeli artists that can lead to later collaborations."[7]

The underlying concept of the *"Hilchot Shchenim, Perek Bet"* (The Laws of Neighbors, Chapter 2) exhibition was similar in its establishment of a creative cooperative of artists across the Middle East and Europe, one that centered on artistic production as a means of art education and public engagement. In this sense, the center began to open up and challenge standard approaches to exhibitions. It did this first by eliminating the exhibition's closing date and replacing it with an open-ended model for continued artistic production. The center also moved the exhibition to another country, allowing for the artistic collaboration of Israeli and Turkish artists about the issues of control, government authority, and the role of the individual to take place outside the borders of Israel and alongside individuals in other, neighboring Arab countries.

A brief survey of the exhibitions at the larger and more established Israel Museum in Jerusalem and Tel Aviv Museum of Art from this same period (2001-2004) reveals a generally conservative array of exhibition subjects that neither responded to the Intifada nor attempted to grapple with its implications.[8] Also in Jerusalem, the Museum on the Seam, located on the border between East and West Jerusalem, created a travelling exhibition entitled *Coexistence* in 2001, which, through publically displayed socio-politically-charged artwork, strove to raise awareness and encourage dialogue regarding issues of religious identity and nationality. But its approach was and still remains vastly different from that of the center's. The Museum on the Seam is a sociopolitical contemporary art museum in Jerusalem that relies on art exhibitions in the public space to "raise controversial social issues for public discussion."[9] Here, 'raising' connotes a passive sense since, for them, the display of art in a public environment or the encounter of an individual with the charged artwork on their gallery walls presents an opportunity for dialogue. However, the actual engagement with the sociopolitical challenges presented is not facilitated or monitored for any sort of impact.

The Center for Digital Art reversed the involvement of the public in their exhibitions, shifting its focus from impacting the public who come to visit and learn about the sociopolitical art on view in a passive way to involving a public that could inform and mold the artwork itself. In other words, active engagement with art and art education began with the art producers themselves. The Center for Digital Art recognized in its artists a type of community or public who would serve as the first responders in a series of art educational models. Their engagement with the art subject and collaboration in the art production represented the first stage in art education: Questioning the meaning of art, challenging the mode of its representation, and struggling with the implications of those decisions on a public or social scale. By creating international collaborative ventures, the center opened up definitions of art, public, and engagement, and it launched a new operating model for long-term impact. Just as the Middle Eastern conflict crossed borders and impacted individuals who were often not given the ability to voice their struggle, so too did the center's new 'international' model of art collaboration, which involved Israeli and non-Israeli artists and venues in exposing and giving voice to individual realities within, or beyond, the conflict.

In 2005, the center launched its *Liminal Spaces* project, an eight-month international art project that brought together artists, academics, architects, and activists to explore "the conflicts, confrontations, and inconspicuous exchange between Jewish and Arab-Palestinian communities in Israel."[10] Nearly derailed by the outbreak of the Second Lebanon War on Israel's northern front in 2006, the project overcame many obstacles to produce an exhibition on the "reality of the occupation."[11] More significant than the exhibition and its international schedule, however, was the realization by the center that the project created a collaborative working model for continued dialogue and engagement on the subject, and that the exhibition "represent[ed] a single step in a longer process."[12] To that end, *Liminal Spaces* was expanded to include workshops for the participants (artists, curators, and cultural figures from Israel and Palestinian Territories and Europe, the UK, and the US) to continue to reflect and debate the subject matter as well as create additional opportunities for individual and group encounters.

It was precisely this idea of utilizing art and art engagement as a means and an end that set the Center for Digital Art apart. Much like the "new public art" model coined by Grant Kester, the center puts into practice a philosophy in which the process of collaboration itself is the focus of the community-based project:

> In this way, the new, community-based public art represents a transition from an earlier model of public art which involved the location of sculptural works in sites administered by public agencies — either federal, state or local governments, or other administrative bodies.[13]

The center began to rapidly expand its rate and scope of activities, doubling its gallery space as it acquired the entire abandoned school complex from the municipality. Internationally, the center was making waves with its "Mobile Archive," launched in 2007 to expand the outreach of its artwork and to establish a "regional cultural network that will become a platform for sharing experiences and ideas."[14] Traveling to more than five international venues in its first year of operation, the "Mobile Archive" was designed as a modular exhibition that allowed hosting institutions to contribute works to the original collection. In this sense, the "Mobile Archive" offered an endless model for potential impact, presenting local sociopolitical artwork alongside others from the Middle East in a continuous pattern of discourse.

Locally, visiting artists, curators, and critics were invited to the center and the city of Holon, to "develop their artistic or theoretical work in relation to our local context."[15] By opening up the 'local context' of Holon for artistic exploration, the Center for Digital Art began to set in motion its innovative model for public art engagement in a local setting.

> We asked ourselves what art could accomplish that rehabilitation, urban welfare, and neighborhood institutions could not. What we saw in our mandate was not to turn the neighborhood into something different, but rather to work from within, to get people out of their crowded homes and improve their daily lives, and together with them, to create a feeling of belonging and involvement.[16]

The Center for Digital Art immediately recognized how Holon's urban renewal program was not succeeding in meeting the needs of the poorer and disenfranchised individuals from the Jesse Cohen neighborhood. The municipality's systematic approach ignored the voices of the residents within the Jesse Cohen neighborhood, sweeping up individuals, each with his or her own histories, opinions, needs, ideas, etc., into a homogenous group. A core value of the center's activities since its inception — and becoming increasingly predominant through its operations and exhibitions — was, as Rosalyn Deutsche explains, "a commitment not only to democracy as a form of government but to a general democratic spirit of equality as well."[17] The failure of the Holon municipality represented a failure of democracy — the ignoring of individual voices and the skewing of their realities. In response, the Center extended its core mission — that of questioning, "how an art institute can reflect and react to volatile conditions of culture and politics and produce a critical approach to the oppressive power of the government" — beyond the gallery walls and into the heart of the community.[18]

Art at the Heart of the Community:
The Jesse Cohen Project

The Jesse Cohen Project was launched by the Center for Digital Art in 2009 to "explore how art can take part in the processes of change on a city or neighborhood scale by working side by side with other municipal, governmental, and private institutions and the tools available to them."[19] Projects are run by the Center for Digital Art in concert with a range of public workers — social workers, educators, teachers, students, business leaders, and volunteers (artists, curators, art activists, and architects). All projects meet the following criteria:

1. They take place in and are comprised of partnerships among the various individuals and agents;

2. They offer long-term impact;

3. They culminate in a final, tangible product.

Jesse Cohen projects begin with a series of meetings between the key figures and organizations, and local residents in order to begin accessing the needs of the local residents. Project leaders do not foist solutions upon the residents; instead, all projects begin with an assessment period wherein residents voice their needs, experiences, ideas, and more. The platform itself, the grouping of interested parties from a range of backgrounds, secures a multidimensional, even pluralistic, approach to the project. Among the guidelines for projects are the following:

> Exploring local knowledge and considering workshops exploring local knowledge transfer between residents; Utilizing open, public spaces and private courtyards; Mediating between the population and "players" in the municipality, government, etc., by the visualization of information, creating an awareness of rights and so on.[20]

Building on infrastructures that already exist — of social workers, welfare systems, and urban planning — the *Jesse Cohen Project* establishes new conditions for dialogue within the current reality. Instead of overturning or working against the city through challenge, protest, or antagonism, the center reframes municipal efforts within a collaborative venture that begins with the needs of the individual and ends with a city and public engaged in their struggle for solutions. Similarly, in a non-challenging approach, Jesse Cohen projects offer an end goal or target completion project that is unrelated to assessments of impact in the neighborhood. In other words, while projects offer concrete solutions or experiences for neighborhood residents, the collaborative process itself is what is monitored for assessing impact. Individuals working together on each project are frequently asked to voice challenges along the way so that the model for collaboration can be addressed during the project itself and repaired for the next one. While long-term impact in the neighborhood is still to be determined, short-term impact from specific projects can be easily garnered by questioning residents for feedback after certain projects are completed. However, this type of long-term impact is secondary in importance to *Jesse Cohen Project* organizers; the real thrust of the impact lies in the bringing together of figures from varying backgrounds to collaborate in working models of community, artistic engagement.

Over the course of 2010 and 2011, the Center for Digital Art, to use Rosalyn Deutsche's assertion, "took democracy seriously," recognizing in the *Jesse Cohen Project* a holistic platform from which it could carry out community-based art projects — by, for and within the community itself.[21] One particular Jesse Cohen project exemplifies the innovative thinking and approaches that typify this initiative.

Design and Social Responsibility, led by Israeli architect and social activist Gil Mualem-Doron, strove to provide neighborhood residents with renovation or interior design changes that would meet the needs of individuals and their families. The planning and design took place over the course of numerous conversations and meetings between architecture and design students from two nearby colleges and neighborhood residents who were interested in participating. Students from the Avni Institute for Art and Design in Tel Aviv met with five families who were interested in redesigning their private apartments, while students from the College for Management Academic Studies in nearby Rishon LeZion met with residents from two specific buildings in the Jesse Cohen neighborhood who were interested in redesigning their shared, communal space. Municipal workers, social workers, and contractors were also involved in the project that often entailed challenging zoning restrictions and redefining tax and building regulations. Plans for the proposed improvements to the apartments were presented in an exhibition while a documentary film also recorded interviews with participants throughout the project.

The College for Management Academic Studies joined the *Jesse Cohen Project* participants and the Center for Digital Art in hosting an international conference in the nearby city of Rishon LeZion on the subject of city, designers, architecture, and civic responsibility. Among the topics discussed was a new 'Designers Clinic' initiative at the College in Rishon LeZion that would approach the field of design, ranging from interior design to industrial design to architecture (or public design), as "not just for the rich, but for everyone. Design that takes upon itself a responsibility to help the weak and find solutions for their needs. Design that takes pride in its ability to create opportunities and not to forcibly reduce them."[22]

In this sense, the project generated several waves of impact: From an individual level, to a community level, to a city level and even a regional, national level.

Reaching beyond the city of Holon itself, the *Jesse Cohen Project* had succeeded in introducing its model of public art engagement for replication in other cities.

On Context and a Continuum of Questioning

"The geo-political reality of the Middle East determines the conditions for cultural and art productions," claims the Center for Digital Art.[23] In other words, the innovative spirit of the Center for Digital Art responds to the contentious conditions that the Middle Eastern conflict dictates both on a national and local level. As Dan Senor and Saul Singer purport, Israeli innovation or creativity,

> is a story not just of talent but of tenacity, of insatiable questioning of authority, of determined informality, combined with a unique attitude toward failure, teamwork, mission, risk and cross-disciplinary creativity.[24]

At key crisis points in the Middle East, the Center for Digital Art responded by reaching beyond borders — of the country, of the community and, most importantly, the museum itself. In the face of adversity — war, closed borders, terror, fear, boycotts, and more — the Center for Digital Art in Holon responded with inventiveness. It opened a context for criticism and engagement among art critics, artists, architects, social activities, educators, and more. It created a new working model for artistic collaboration both in Israel and around the world, one that rose above the conflicts raging within Israel to examine sociopolitical issues from multiple perspectives — individual, community, nation, country. And, in doing so, it unearthed a new space for civic engagement — the community — recognizing therein the potential for art education and education through a broadly defined art: as a method of production, as a cultural process and approach, and as a discourse. In liberating art from the museum walls, the Center for Digital Art broke with traditional practices, symbolic of enforced borders or governmental policies. Tapping into a "set of highly attenuated prisms,"[25] as Irit Rogoff calls it, the center founded a new conversational or interactive approach and practice for public art engagement, one that involves a range of collaborators (artists, social workers, scientists, city planners, economists, etc.) in the issues of the day.

Driving into the city of Holon, through its main entrance, bright red navigational signs in English, Hebrew, and Arabic direct and herald visitors to the many new museums across the city's developing southern area. Conveying a sense of urgency in their emergency red and yellow coloring, it is hard to ignore their appeal: museums for children, design, cartoons and caricatures, cultural centers, and theaters among them. Continue past this blaring plea for attention, however, and a small, Hebrew-only sign will quietly point to the lesser-known Israel Center for Digital Art. Upon mentioning this to the Director and Chief Curator of the Center for Digital Art Eyal Danon, he answers, "Yes, it bothers me a lot. More at first actually, but then again, we're not a museum, so maybe that's why." Grappling with sociopolitical artwork, the Center for Digital Art began to unpack the meanings and structures of museums, their roles vis-à-vis the public, the methods and value of art education, and the potential for sociopolitical discourse on a public level. By leaving the museum and venturing into the surrounding community, the Center for Digital Art in Holon recognized the potentiality of art education as a process and platform for art engagement in the widest and deepest possible terms.

Notes

1. Holon municipality. Accessed December 25, 2011. http://holon.muni.il/English/Pages/default.aspx.
2. Ami Ran, "The Parks of Holon as a Parablet," Architecture of Israel Quarterly, 36. http://www.aiq.co.il/pages/EnglishArticle.asp?id=48.
3. Liat Levi, "Crime, Drugs and Neglect: The Story of Jesse Cohen," Maariv, 19 July 2010. Hebrew article.
4. Interview with Eyal Danon, Project Space Survival Strategies, Accessed November 5, 2011. http://invisiblevenue.typepad.com/project_space_survey/digital-art-lab.html.
5. Center for Digital Art. Accessed April 1, 2011. http://www.digitalartlab.org.il/ExhibitionPage.asp?id=54&path=level_1.
6. Center for Digital Art. Accessed December 15, 2011. http://www.digitalartlab.org.il/ExhibitionPage.asp?id=53&path=level_1.
7. Center for Digital Art. Accessed April 1, 2012. http://www.digitalartlab.org.il/ExhibitionPage.asp?id=53&path=level_1.
8. The listings of exhibitions of these years on the websites of both the Israel Museum, Jerusalem and the Tel Aviv Museum of Art, from the years 2001–2004, detailed dozens of art exhibitions, but only two could be connected to a sociopolitical context or subject. And that's because they are contemporary art exhibitions that address contemporary issues but do not respond to or address directly issues of the Intifada conflict. Accessed January 5, 2012. http://www.imj.org.il/exhibitions/presentation/ and http://www.tamuseum.com/exhibition-category/current-exhibitions.
9. Museum on the Seam. Accessed December 25, 2011. http://www.mots.org.il.
10. Liminal Spaces. Accessed November 7, 2011. http://liminalspaces.org/.
11. Liminal Spaces. Accessed November 7, 2011. http://liminalspaces.org/.
12. Liminal Spaces. Accessed November 7, 2011. http://liminalspaces.org/.
13. Grant H. Kester, "Aesthetic Evangelists: Conversion and Empowerment in Contemporary Community Art," Afterimage 22 (January 1995) 1.
14. Center for Digital Art. Accessed December 15, 2011. http://www.digitalartlab.org.il/ExhibitionPage.asp?id=408&path=level_1.
15. Center for Digital Art. Accessed December 15, 2011.
16. "Architecture for the People, by the People," Accessed January 20, 2012. http://sizedoesntmatter.com/culture/architecture-by-the-people-for-the-people/.

17. Rosalyn Deutsche, "Art and Public Space: Questions of Democracy," Social Text 33 (1992). Accessed November 16, 2011. Http://www.jstor.org/stable/466433.
18. Center for Digital Art. Accessed December 15, 2011.
19. Jesse Cohen Project. Accessed November 7, 2011. www.jessy.digitalartlab.org.il.
20. Jesse Cohen Project. Accessed November 7, 2011. www.jessy.digitalartlab.org.il.
21. Rosalyn Deutsche, "Art and Public Space: Questions of Democracy," Social Text 33 (1992) 34. Accessed November 16, 2011. Http://www.jstor.org/stable/466433.
22. Newsletter. Quoted by Carmela Yakobi Volk, Head of Interior Design Unit at the College of Management Academic Studies, Rishon Lezion. My translation. Accessed January 15, 2012. http://www.colman.ac.il/ABOUT/NEWS/Pages/design_and_social_responsibility_1_2011.aspx.
23. Center for Digital Art. Accessed December 15, 2011. http://www.digitalartlab.org.il/ExhibitionPage.asp?id=408&path=level_1.
24. Dan Senor and Saul Singer, Start-Up Nation: The Story of Israel's Economic Miracle, (New York: Twelve, 2009), 18.
25. Irit Rogoff, "Turning," eflux, November 2008. http://www.eflux.com/journal/turning/.

About the Author

Ziva Haller Rubenstein is a freelance writer and researcher of Israeli arts and culture for newspapers and leading websites including her own blog, Designist Dream. She has a B.A. in Art History from Barnard College and an M.A. in Art History and Museum Studies Certificate from Tufts University. She moved to Israel in 2000 after working in museums and art organizations in the US and UK.

Exploring Staff Facilitation that Supports Family Learning

Scott A. Pattison and Lynn D. Dierking

Abstract Front-line educators are arguably critical to the visitor experience at museums and science centers across the country. However, little research exists to inform staff facilitation strategies or professional development efforts. In this article, we describe the results of a qualitative study of 63 staff-family interactions in a science center, focusing particularly on the role of adult family members. We observed three distinct phases of interaction, during which adult family members acted as gatekeepers to deeper staff engagement. The results suggest that in order to successfully facilitate family learning, museum educators must carefully consider the role of adults and the unique social context of museums learning.

Introduction

There is growing recognition that museums and science centers are an important part of the educational infrastructure of our communities, with a long history of offering engaging learning experiences through exhibitions, staff-facilitated activities and programs, and community outreach.[1] Fueled by the recognition that front-line museum educators[2] can play a powerful role in supporting learning in these settings, there has been increased interest in the last decade for supporting staff-mediated experiences.[3] In response, a number of institutions have created professional development programs for their front-line educators.

Despite growing interest, however, there is little research on the characteristics of successful staff-mediated learning to inform the work of these educators or ground professional development efforts.[4] Although some researchers have investigated highly structured museum programs, such as school group tours,[5]

Journal of Museum Education, Volume 37, Number 3, Fall 2012, pp. 69–80.

demonstrations,[6] and museum theatre,[7] it is not clear whether these findings inform the vast number of unstructured interactions, or unscripted conversations between staff and visitors mediated by exhibitions or educational activities, that are regularly a part of the museum experience.

To address this gap and inform professional development efforts, we conducted a study of unstructured staff-family interactions at the Oregon Museum of Science and Industry (OMSI), Portland, Oregon. Because so little is known, the research was necessarily broad and exploratory, designed to lay a foundation for future studies of the impact of staff facilitation on family learning. Three research questions guided the investigation:

1. What is the nature of unstructured interactions between museum staff and family groups at OMSI?

2. How do staff members and family groups initiate unstructured interactions?

3. How do families and staff negotiate roles and relationships during unstructured interactions?

The study built on two notable exceptions to the dearth of research on unstructured staff-visitor interactions: a mixed-method study of zoo educators and a qualitative study of living history museum interpreters.[8] Mony and Heimlich (2008) found that the length of interactions and the number of educational messages communicated were influenced by visitor group composition and how interactions were initiated, with staff- adult group interactions being longer with more educational messages. Interactions also lasted longer when staff approached visitors, although the number of messages was similar. Although the sample size was small, Rosenthal and Blankman-Hetrick (2002) found that staff facilitation prompted families to engage in more learning conversations subsequent to interactions. Findings from both of these studies indicate that the ways in which staff facilitation interacts with the social context of family learning may be important to understanding the nature and outcomes of these interactions.

This study was also framed within everyday social interaction and sociolinguistics literature. Such research has rarely been applied to the study of behavior and learning in free-choice settings but offers insights into the rules and patterns that govern everyday interactions, and likely shape unstructured staff-visitor interactions.[9] Findings highlight the importance of opening sequences such as greetings; the negotiation of roles and relationships; and nonverbal communication.[10] More generally, this body of literature suggests that understanding the social nature of staff-family interactions (the "how") may be as critical as investigating the educational content of staff-facilitated activities and programs (the "what").

The full results of the study are reported elsewhere.[11] This article specifically explores the central role that adult family members played during unstructured staff-family interactions.

Methods

As noted above, the present study was exploratory and qualitative, focusing particularly on describing the nature of staff-visitor interactions and uncovering themes and patterns that might inform practice and future research.[12] To collect data, we video and audio taped un-cued interactions between staff (both paid staff and volunteers) and families in two learning labs, the Physics Lab and the Chemistry Lab, at the Oregon Museum of Science and Industry (OMSI), Portland, Oregon, over the course of four days, between May 30 and June 6, 2010. Both labs offer visitors opportunities to engage more deeply with scientific activities and phenomena and were specifically designed to support structured and unstructured staff-visitor interactions. In consultation with OMSI educators, we chose activities that were popular with both visitors and staff members and represented a range of activity types, from a lengthy, visitor-directed chemistry experiment to a stand-alone, phenomenon-based physics activity. To preserve the authentic nature of interactions, visitors and staff were not actively recruited to participate in the study. Instead, signage notified visitors that videotaping was in progress, following methods developed by the Exploratorium.[13]

Appropriate to our qualitative approach, we did not analyze the data using predefined categories. Rather, our analysis identified themes and patterns that emerged from the recorded interactions, informed by concepts from the literature described above. In total we collected data for 63 interactions between staff and families (defined as intergenerational groups that included at least one visitor over and one under the age of 18). During later rounds of analysis, we specifically focused on a subset of 33 interactions in order to balance the representation of settings, activities, and staff members.

Results

Our analysis of the videotaped interactions revealed three themes:
- Interactions were characterized by three distinct phases of role and goal negotiation between staff members and adult visitors: initiating the interaction, facilitating the activity, and introducing new learning goals.

- During each phase, adult family members acted as gatekeepers to deeper staff involvement. Without the support of adults, it was difficult for staff members to establish themselves as learning facilitators for family groups.
- The physical and social contexts of the interactions either supported or inhibited staff members' abilities to engage with families.

Phases of Staff-Family Interactions

Viewed through a social interaction lens (the "how"), rather than a transmission of content perspective (the "what"), interactions between families and staff members involved an ongoing process of role and goal negotiation, with staff members working to establish themselves as meaningful participants in family interactions and attempting to influence the nature and goals of those interactions. During the initial phase of interaction, we observed that staff members and volunteers used a variety of strategies to introduce themselves to families and define their role as a potential learning facilitator, including greeting visitors, inviting them to participate in an activity, asking check-in questions, offering guidance or tips, or simply inserting themselves into a conversation or interaction.

When staff members persisted through the initiation phase, interactions often became focused on facilitating family learning. During this second phase, both staff members and adult visitors were highly involved in facilitating, guiding and directing activities, interpreting scientific phenomenon and content, helping to focus attention, modeling and demonstrating, and offering encouragement to their children. In almost every case we observed, adult family members maintained an active leadership role during interactions, despite the presence of museum educators. In some instances, adults used many of the same facilitation strategies as the educators, while in others, they adopted different, but complementary roles, talking or answering for the group, restating staff comments and suggestions, or playing a parental role by managing family members. Adults used a variety of strategies to assert their knowledge and expertise during interactions with staff members, including being an active co-facilitator, sharing stories and anecdotes that highlighted their own knowledge and experiences, answering knowingly to staff comments, and even on a few occasions completing the sentences of staff members.

Frequently, staff members not only supported family learning, but tried to shift the focus of the family activity. In this third phase, staff members introduced new learning goals, such as understanding the science behind the activity or phenomenon, even if the family was using the activity in a playful way or problem solving manner. Adult family members also introduced new goals, but this strategy was much more common with staff members. For example, at a musical glasses activity in the Physics lab, where families explored making musical tones with different sizes and shapes of glasses, staff members frequently used props to demonstrate how the tones were generated by the vibrations of the glass, shifting the purpose of the activity from exploration of musical aesthetics to understanding the science of sound and vibrations. As was observed during initiation, the introduction of new learning goals by staff highlighted the important role of adult family members, who often responded quite clearly, either supporting or blocking the new direction suggested by the staff members. The three phases of staff-visitor interactions are summarized in Table 1.

Table 1 Three phases of unstructured staff-visitor interactions.

Phase	Description	Adult Roles
Initiating the interaction	Staff members engage with families and attempt to establish a role as learning facilitators.	Adults communicate (verbally or nonverbally) either a willingness or non-willingness to engage with staff members; interactions without adult support are often brief or characterized by ongoing tension.
Facilitating the activity	Staff members and adult visitors use a variety of strategies to support family learning and engagement.	Adults work to maintain leadership roles during interactions by directly facilitating family learning, co-facilitating with staff members, and communicating their knowledge and expertise.
Introducing new learning goals	Staff members, and occasionally adult visitors, suggest a new focus for the activity, such as a switch from free exploration to understanding the scientific phenomenon.	Adults evaluate the appropriateness of the new learning goal for their families; adults then communicate (verbally or nonverbally) either a willingness or non-willingness to support the new goal.

Adults as Gatekeepers

Reviewing the videotaped interactions, we consistently observed that adult family members played the role of gatekeepers, using subtle (and occasionally, not so subtle) verbal and nonverbal cues to signal their willingness to have staff participate in the family activity. Without the support of adult family members, it was extremely difficult for staff members to establish connections with families or meaningfully facilitate learning.

This important role of adult family members was particularly noticeable when staff members attempted to initiate the interaction or introduce new learning goals. For example, during the initiation phase, we observed adult family members responding to the arrival of staff by either fully acknowledging them, such as looking up, smiling, and politely responding to a staff member's question, or only partially acknowledging them, such as looking at them without verbally responding or verbally responding but not looking at them. In a few cases, adult family members ignored staff altogether. Although the difference between these responses was subtle, it appeared to have a strong influence on the subsequent nature of the interactions. When adults partially acknowledged or ignored staff members, interactions were usually brief or characterized by ongoing tension. In other cases, in which adult family members fully acknowledged staff members, educators were able to engage more meaningfully with visitor groups. This was

Unstructured interaction between a family and a museum educator in OMSI's Physics Lab. Photo by Scott Pattison.

also true in the few examples where staff members had a very clear role from the beginning of the interaction, such as when a staff member had already engaged a child at an activity station and the parent approached later. Social interaction research suggests that establishing clear roles and relationships is a necessary prerequisite for any meaningful social interaction.[14] Interestingly, among the interactions we observed that were initiated by staff, adult family members fully acknowledged staff initiation only about half of the time.

We observed similar dynamics when staff members attempted to introduce new learning goals. Without adult support, families rarely followed the lead of staff members. Adults seemed particularly quick to respond when family members, and especially young children, were not engaged by the new focus suggested by staff members. For example, at the musical glasses activity described above, the father remarked, "Yeah, I think he just wants to hear the sounds," when the educator was attempting to explain the vibration of the glass to him and his son. Of the interactions we observed, adult family members supported about half of the new learning goals staff members introduced. These findings suggest that the introduction of new learning goals by staff members may have threatened adults' roles as facilitators of family learning. The role of adult family members during each phase of the interactions is summarized in Table 1.

Importance of Physical and Social Context

Our analysis of the videotaped interactions also highlighted the important influence of physical and social context on staff-family interactions. Both the overall design of the learning labs and the specific exhibits or activities offered different tools, as well as different constraints, during each phase of the interactions. For example, in the Chemistry Lab, the activity stations were oriented so that families could establish their own, distinct space and included all the necessary supplies and instructions for a successful experience. Family members frequently used the activity instructions as a tool for claiming knowledge and expertise during the interaction or to contest new learning goals introduced by staff members.

In contrast, the Physics Lab created a much more staff-oriented experience. Many of the activities did not have clear visitor instructions or clearly defined spaces for families to gather. For instance, at one activity, staff members often sat at the counter and invited families to participate, creating a much clearer role for educators. At another exhibit, it was possible to stand around all sides of the activity, creating natural spaces for staff members to engage with families. Staff members appeared to use the lack of instructional text, as well as a variety of additional staff-only props, to help establish their roles and assert their knowledge and expertise. Interestingly, ignoring or only partially acknowledging staff initiation was more common in the Chemistry Lab compared to the Physics Lab. Also, educators were much more likely to invite families to participate in an activity in the Physics Lab compared to the Chemistry Lab.

We also observed that the social context was an important influence on staff-family interactions. In general, any social circumstance that helped to more clearly define a staff member's role seemed to support longer and/or more satisfying staff-family interactions. For example, in the Physics Lab, all of the cases of successful staff initiation occurred when a family was initially confused about how to begin the activity or use the exhibit. Because of the clear need, adults in these examples were very willing to support staff members' roles. Adults also appeared to be very willing to engage with staff members when staff had already begun facilitating an activity for children in the family group. In the Chemistry Lab, a similar dynamic was created when adults, prompted by the instructions at the end of one of the lab experiments, asked staff members to perform a short demonstration. In fact, the overwhelming majority of visitor-initiated interactions occurred because visitors were prompted by instructions, perhaps suggesting that without explicit prompting, families may either be unaware of the role that staff members can play as learning facilitators or may prefer to experience the activities on their own.

Implications for Museum Educators

Study findings highlight unstructured staff-family interactions as challenging contexts for front-line museum educators, embodying all the complexity of everyday social interaction. Although more research is needed to understand how the patterns of staff-visitor interactions observed in this study transfer to other settings and visitor groups, the findings reinforce much of what we know from studies of family learning in museums more generally. For example, one of the most robust findings from the visitor studies and museum research is that adults play an important role in facilitating family learning in museums.[15] Prior research also indicates that adult visitors come to museums with identities, motivations, and goals of their own, including a desire to facilitate learning for other family members, which shape the nature and outcomes of their visits.[16] Given this research, it is not surprising that we found that adults played a strong role even in the presence of museum educators, and that these adults used a variety of strategies to maintain and support their role as learning facilitators for their families.

Based on both prior family research and the results of this exploratory study, we make the following preliminary recommendations to support front-line educators successfully facilitating unstructured interactions with families:

1. **Managers and supervisors should become familiar with family learning research and build on this literature when developing facilitation techniques, programs, and staff training.** They should also consider the complex role negotiation and social dynamics inherent in unstructured staff-family interactions when training paid and unpaid front-line museum educators. Although leading large group demonstrations and classroom programs is often considered a higher level skill in the museum education field, it may be that facilitating unstructured family learning is equally, if not more, challenging for new staff members.

2. **Front-line museum educators should adopt facilitation approaches that recognize and support the unique role that adults play in family learning in museums.** These approaches should leverage the deep understanding parents and caregivers often have of their families' knowledge, interests, and prior learning experiences, as well as adult family members' natural inclination to facilitate successful learning experiences for their families.

3. **Designers, exhibit developers, and front-line educators should work together to create learning environments that take into account the role of educational staff as they attempt to support family learning in respectful ways that leverage on-going interactions of families.** In many cases, the design of the physical context may be just as critical to supporting successful staff-family interactions as the strategies used by front-line educators.

An Example of Applying Research to Practice

As part of the National Science Foundation-funded *Access Algebra* exhibition and professional development project, front-line educators, exhibit designers, and evaluators at OMSI have worked together to begin putting many of these recommendations into action. The overarching goal of the exhibition, called *Design Zone*, is to engage visitors in exploring the mathematics underlying the creative and design arts, including music, engineering, computer programming, and visual design. From the beginning of the project, exhibit developers and designers were committed to working with front-line educators to create exhibit activities and physical spaces within the exhibition to specifically support staff-family interactions. Building on the work of Sue Allen and her colleagues at the

Exploratorium,[17] the project team termed these design elements "facilitation affordances," highlighting the ways that the physical design of activities could purposefully enhance the ability of staff to facilitate family learning. Examples in the final exhibition include props stored in locked cabinets available only to front-line educators; operating modes for electronic or computer-based activities that can be activated by front-line educators to either help deepen visitor engagement or eliminate feedback that might interfere with staff-family interactions; and physical elements designed to create comfortable spaces for front-line educators to stand without intruding on visitor interactions.

Team members also worked together to test approaches for staff-facilitated family math learning in the exhibition. Through formative testing, the team identified four broad categories of staff facilitation strategies — orienting, posing challenges, promoting math talk, and supporting visitor interactions — as promising approaches to deepen visitor engagement and empower visitors. Posing challenges seemed to be a particularly successful and nonthreatening way for front-line educators to guide family groups. Providing visitors with a challenge gave them a common goal and created the potential for exciting, memorable experiences. Adult visitors often reiterated and helped facilitate the challenges for their families. Evaluation results suggest the approach is a promising technique for leveraging, rather than inhibiting, the important role adults in the family are often eager to play.

Conclusion

This is an exciting time for museum education. With increased attention on informal learning experiences and the role of front-line museum educators, the community is in a strong position to improve the science and practice of museum education. However, we cannot make progress without a serious commitment to examining, studying, reflecting on, and improving our own practice. We must have strong, empirical evidence to support our claim that front-line educators are important, even essential, to the role that museums play as facilitators of lifelong, informal learning, and advocate on their behalf and in partnership with them. In particular these findings suggest that front-line educators need training and mentoring that focuses on noticing and responding to the nuanced behavior of families. We hope this study has made a small contribution to this effort and helps to set the stage for future studies and meaningful educator-researcher collaborations.

Acknowledgments

We are grateful to all the staff and volunteers at the Oregon Museum of Science and Industry who supported or participated in this research. Special thanks go to Michael Alaniz, Marcie Benne, Elizabeth Dannen, Annie Gilbert, Michelle Herrmann, and Craig Reed. Thanks also to the many *Access Algebra* team members and project partners, including Jennifer Bachman, Karyn Bertschi, Mary Kay Cunningham, Michael Dalton, Scott Ewing, Jan Mokros, David Perry, and Andee Rubin, who inspired us throughout this project.

Notes

1. J. Falk, M. Storksdieck, and L. Dierking, "Investigating public science interest and understanding: Evidence for the importance of free-choice learning," *Public Understanding of Science* 16 (2007): 455–469. National Research Council, *Learning science in informal environments: People-places, and pursuits.* (Washington, DC: The National Academies Press, 2009). US Department of Education, *Report of the Academic Competitiveness Council* (Washington, DC: US Department of Education, 2007).

2. Throughout this article, we use the terms front-line educator and museum educator to refer to paid and unpaid staff who work in museums, science centers, and other informal or free-choice learning environments and whose primary responsibility is to facilitate learning experiences for visitors, including families, adults, seniors, and school groups.

3. T. Astor-Jack et al., "Understanding the complexities of socially-mediated learning," in *In principle, in practice: Museums as learning institutions*, ed. by J. Falk, L. Dierking, and S. Foutz, 217–228, Lanham, MD: AltaMira Press, 2007. National Research Council, *Learning science in informal environments*.

4. T. Astor-Jack et al., "Understanding the complexities of socially-mediated learning," 217–228. John Falk and Lynn Dierking, *Learning from museums: Visitor experiences and the making of meaning* (New York: AltaMira Press, 2000). National Research Council, *Learning science in informal environments*.

5. U. Anderson et al., "Enhancing the zoo visitor's experience by public animal training and oral interpretation at an otter exhibit," *Environment and Behavior* 35 (2003): 826–841. A. Cox-Peterson et al., "Investigation of guided school tours, student learning, and science reform recommendations at a museum of natural history," *Journal of Research in Science Teaching* 40 (2003): 200–218. B. Flexer and M. Borun, "The impact of a class visit to a participatory science museum exhibit in a classroom science lesson," *Journal of Research in Science Teaching* 21(1984): 863–873. T. Jarvis and A. Pell, "Factors influencing elementary school children's attitudes toward science before, during, and after a visit to the UK National Space Center," *Journal of Research in Science Teaching* 42 (2005): 53–83. T. Tal and O. Morag, "School visits to natural history museums: Teaching or enriching?" *Journal of Research in Science Teaching* 44 (2007): 747 769. L. Tran, "Teaching science in museums: The pedagogy and goals of museum educators," *Science Education* 91 (2006): 1–21.

6. D. Anderson et al., "Children's museum experiences: Identifying powerful mediators of learning," *Curator* 45 (2002): 213–231.

7. T. Bridal, *Exploring Museum Theatre* (Walnut Creek, CA: AltaMira Press, 2004). C. Hughes, *Museum Theatre: Communicating with Visitors through Drama* (Portsmouth, NH: Heinemann, 1998).

8. P. Mony and J. Heimlich, "Talking to visitors about conservation: Exploring message communication through docent-visitor interactions at zoos," *Visitor Studies* 11 (2008): 151–162. E. Rosenthal and J. Blankman-Hetrick, "Conversations across time: Family learning in a living history museum," In *Learning conversations in museums*, ed. by G. Leinhardt, K. Crowley, and K. Knutson (Mahwah, NJ: Lawrence Erlbaum Associates, 2002).

9. D. vom Lehn, C. Heath, and J. Hindmarsh, "Exhibiting interaction: Conduct and collaboration in museums and galleries," *Symbolic Interaction* 24 (2001): 189–216.

10. For example: L. Filliettaz, "Mediated actions, social practices, and contextualization: A case study from service encounters," In *Discourse in action: Introducing mediated discourse analysis*, ed. by S. Norris & R. Jones (London: Routledge, 2005), 100–09. E. Goffman, *The presentation of self in everyday life* (New York: Anchor Books, 1959). E. Goffman, *Interaction ritual* (New York: Anchor Books, 1967). J. Gumperz and D. Hymes, eds., *Directions in sociolinguistics: The ethnography of communication* (New York: Holt, Reinhart, and Winston, 1972). S. Rowe, "Using multiple situation definitions to create hybrid activity space," *In Discourse in action: Introducing mediated discourse analysis*, ed. by S. Norris & R. Jones (London: Routledge, 2005), 123–134. R. Scollon, *Mediated discourse as social interaction: A study of news discourse* (New York: Longman, 1998). J. Wertsch, *Mind as action* (New York: Oxford University Press, 1998).

11. S. Pattison and L. Dierking, *Staff-mediated learning in museums: A social interaction perspective* (manuscript in review, 2012).

12. K. Charmaz, *Constructing grounded theory: A practical guide through qualitative analysis* (Thousand Oaks, CA: Sage Publications, 2006). J. Lofland, J. "Analytic ethnography," *Journal of Contemporary Ethnography* 24 (1995): 30–67. C. Marshall and G. Rossman, *Designing qualitative research* (Thousand Oaks, CA: Sage Publications, 2006).

13. J. Gutwill, "Gaining visitor consent for research II: Improving the posted-sign method," *Curator* 46 (2003): 228–235.

14. Scollon, *Mediated discourse as social interaction*.

15. For example: K. Crowley et al., "Shared scientific thinking in everyday parent-child activity," *Science Education* 85 (2001): 712–732. K. Crowley and S. Palmquist, "From teachers to testers: How parents talk to novice and expert children in a natural history museum," *Science Education* 91 (2007), 783–804. J. Fender and K. Crowley, "How parent explanation changes what children learn from everyday scientific thinking," *Journal of Applied Developmental Psychology* 28 (2007): 189–210. M. Gleason and L. Schauble, "Parents' assistance of their children's scientific reasoning," *Cognition and Instruction* 17 (2000): 343–378.

16. J. Falk, *Identity and the museum experience* (Walnut Creek, CA: Left Coast Press, 2009).

17. S. Allen, "Exhibit design in science museums: Dealing with a constructivist dilemma," In *In principle, in practice*, ed. by In J. Falk, L. Dierking, and S. Foutz (Lanham, MD: AltaMira Press, 2007), 43–56.

About the Authors

Scott Pattison is a researcher and evaluator at the Oregon Museum of Science and Industry, Portland, Oregon, and a doctoral student at Oregon State University. His work focuses broadly on helping museums to engage with their communities and address critical issues in science, technology, engineering, and mathematics (STEM) education.

Lynn D. Dierking is Sea Grant Professor in Free-Choice STEM Learning, College of Science and Interim Associate Dean for Research, College of Education, Oregon State University. Her research involves lifelong learning, particularly free-choice, out-of-school time learning (in after-school, home, community-based and cultural contexts), with a focus on youth, families, and community, particularly those under-represented in science.

Creating Chicago History

Making Outreach Craft Activities Meaningful

Madeline Karp

Abstract   When it comes to having a traveling outreach activity for a museum, a craft can seem like the perfect solution. It can seemingly be all things at once— educational, quick and fun. But, if poorly constructed, crafts can also have serious fallbacks. Using the Chicago History Museum and the Millennium Park Family Fun Festival as a case study, this article discusses what goes into designing an effective craft, and how museums can make the most of crafting at an outreach event.

The assignment was simple: Design three crafts that visitors could make outside in the park. Be sure the crafts represented the mission and collection of the Chicago History Museum (CHM). Make them more involved than coloring, but do not use paint, glitter or call for the extensive use of scissors. Produce interesting crafts, original to CHM. Simple.

When it comes to having a mobile activity for a museum, a craft can seem like the perfect solution. It's artistic, it's fast, and it can be repeated in a pinch at future events. But can a craft be the "everyman" of activities — simultaneously be educational, represent the museum's mission and teach the visitor something about city history? The answer is yes — if the craft and craft environment are carefully constructed. Creating a craft for a museum outreach program is not nearly as easy as it sounds. It requires museum professionals to delicately balance history education with kinetic activity, all while leaving plenty of room for individual creativity and fun. Using the Chicago History Museum's participation in the Millennium Park Family Fun Festival as a case study, this article will discuss what museums can do to make crafts truly effective.

Journal of Museum Education, Volume 37, Number 3, Fall 2012, pp. 81–90.

Challenges and Goals at Millennium Park

The Millennium Park Family Fun Festival is a summer-long celebration of the arts, hosted in a wedding tent in the heart of downtown Chicago. Programming during the summer of 2011 included daily musical and theatrical performances, sponsored storytelling hours, and activity stations where children were encouraged to build with blocks, play with hula hoops and make crafts. In 2011 the city of Chicago invited CHM and nine other museums to host an arts and crafts table inside the tent for one week each. Institutional crafts needed to be appropriate for children ages five and up, with a focus on grades three through five.

While the festival's goals were fairly straightforward, the education interns and staffers at the Chicago History Museum outlined a few extra, institutional goals:

1. **Encourage tent visitors to learn something new about Chicago's history.**

2. **Promote the museum to the public.** In 2004, the museum changed its name from the Chicago Historical Society to the Chicago History Museum, creating brand confusion. We especially wanted to reiterate basic information like the museum's location and basic exhibit content.

3. **Relate our crafts back to the museum's collections, exhibits and programs.** The festival provided an opportunity to reach out to a new demographic. With "cool" crafts connected directly to an object on display or an upcoming program, we could entice tent visitors to come to the museum.

Creating a Craft

Anna Reyner of Early Childhood News asserts that there is a distinct difference between an *art* activity and a *craft* activity. While both arts and crafts require guided instruction, art activities develop emotional expression, are process oriented, require basic materials and have limited instructions. Art is open-ended. Craft activities, on the other hand, have a specific end result, but allow for creative process in getting there. Crafts develop critical thinking, coordination, sequencing and relational skills — all of which are essential to developing an understanding of and appreciation for history.[1] To make sure our activity met all goals, we needed to make sure it fell firmly into the *craft* component of arts and crafts.

When constructed properly, crafts can have a big influence on whether a child becomes interested in — and remembers — historical content. Daniel Spock of the Minnesota Historical Society maintains that children learn through sensory experiences, and that an authentic, immersive experience can have a profound impact on how a child learns.[2] For children, experience is informative. Research has shown that people — and children in particular — only remember half of what they hear and read, but remember up to 70% of what they say, and an astonishing 90% percent of what they do.[3] This idea of "doing" informed the Chicago History Museum's understanding of what a craft needed to be; instead of helping *teach* history, the craft needed to make history. The kids visiting were not necessarily *learning* history; they were *creating* it.

This idea sounds a little unusual, but the paradox is exactly what can make history appealing to a child. For adults, history is taught from preserved objects, and documents indexed and passed down. In comparison, making history — inserting oneself into an historical narrative through creative enterprise — can sound like a disrespectful exercise, especially when dealing with serious historical events. Since history often deals with weighty subjects, the gravitas that would attract an adult can easily alienate a child. Adults often dismiss crafts as novel; however it is the novelty of the craft that is so appealing to a child and can make history come alive.

Crafts and Historical Interpretation

In *Never Too Young to Connect to History*, Sharon Shaffer, executive director of the Smithsonian's Early Enrichment Center, writes: "A child's ability to connect to the past and construct meaning [from it]. . . is qualitatively different from that of an adult."[4] History is a cut and dry concept for children. Where an adult uses historical interpretation to formulate a larger narrative and construct societal meaning, a child sees history as anything that has already happened. It is simply a way to sequence past events. Additionally, children's understanding of history is often deeply related to personal experience. For example, as a child reaches age four or five, she begins to understand that history is marked by important past events, but in her construction, history is only that which has happened to her, her family or her friends. Therefore, a young child is more likely to understand history in terms of herself — past birthdays, new school years, vacations, and holidays are the height of history.[5]

So, to ask a child to find personal meaning in an event like the Great Chicago Fire of 1871 was completely out of the question. Children under ten cannot make such abstract connections. Instead of talking about the Great Fire specifically, the craft needed to instead ask children to think about fire in *general*. Through this line of inquiry, volunteers and educators were able to tie the child's experience with fire into the bigger concept of the Great Fire. For example, if a child drew a picture of herself at a campfire, the educator could begin a conversation about things that melt in fires.

- Do marshmallows melt in fires?
- What happens to a candle when you light it?
- If something melts, does it need to be really hot, or really cold?

This simple line of inquiry can lead to a conversation about — and imagining — unusual things that melted during the Great Fire, as a result of the extreme temperature of the flames.[6]

Keeping the questions simple proved to be an important element for the educators and volunteers as well. Of the 49 people working the event, only nine were education staff members or department interns. The other 40 participants were a mix of volunteers, docents and staffers or interns from a variety of departments including Visitors Services, Marketing, IT and even the President's Office. Eight to ten volunteers worked each day — with four or five taking a morning shift, and four or five in the afternoon — but there was no guarantee that any of the volunteers scheduled for a given shift knew Chicago's history. Though we did not have time to give a crash course in history during the hour-long orientation sessions prior to the event, we did stress that everyone was considered an educator for the day and should take the role seriously. Encouraging the volunteers and staffers to keep questions simple — When did the World's Fair happen? How many baseball teams does Chicago have? — increased the likelihood that staffers from other departments could teach visitors about Chicago and Chicago history. We suggested tent volunteers try to steer the conversation towards something about which they knew, but made clear that the educators and education interns could easily be called over to answer questions when volunteers had a moment of doubt, or sincerely did not know the answer. We maintained an unspoken "no embarrassment" policy — no one should feel embarrassed about not knowing something, it was okay to be honest with visitors about not knowing the answer, and asking an educator was always better than making something up.

Choosing Crafts and Craft Materials

As mentioned earlier, CHM needed to have three different crafts for the festival. Variation in the crafts would keep interest high, and allow the team to tackle several historical themes at once. To brainstorm we asked:

- What are some of CHM's most interesting artifacts?
- What periods of history are children interested in?
- What kinds of crafts are gender-neutral and age appropriate?
- What history are they most likely to learn between third and fifth grade?
- Does the history curriculum vary depending on where you live, or what kind of school you attend?[7]

Based on the answers, we began to cross-reference craft ideas, interesting artifacts, relevant historical periods and the learning styles of third, fourth and fifth graders. We came up with three crafts: A bookmark, a "Sweet Home Chicago" mobile, and a Great Chicago Fire pencil topper. I will primarily discuss the bookmark, as it was the easiest craft to reproduce, and the most successful of the week.

The bookmark's success stemmed from its utility. Making a paper lantern celebrating the museum's *My Chinatown* exhibit might be fun, but it wouldn't provide enough opportunity to teach about Chicago history. The craft would likely be hung in a window only to be thrown away within a few weeks. Having such a disposable craft was counter-active, because we imagined people throwing away their crafts as a metaphor for throwing away our lesson — the longer a craft's shelf life at home, the longer the visitor would be reminded of the festival, CHM, and Chicago history.

So, bookmarks proved to have several favorable qualities. In addition to being one of the visitors' favorite crafts of the summer, bookmarks could inspire children to read, and to read specifically about Chicago city history. CHM has a webpage dedicated entirely to "Great Chicago Stories."[8] To encourage visitors to check out the website and read about Chicago, we listed popular stories and GCS's web address on the back of each bookmark. By giving the visitors "Chicago-style" summer reading ideas, we felt we were improving the longevity of our bookmarks, prolonging the visitors' interest in CHM and Chicago history.

The bookmarks granted children extraordinary control over the craft. The front of the bookmark had one instruction: "Leave Your Mark on History" Children working on the craft had complete control over the bookmark's content and design. According to Blanche Jefferson, former Chairman of Art Education at the University of Pittsburgh, having a broad topic for an artistic project (like "Chicago history") encourages the child to use his imagination, tap into a wide range of emotions and ideas, and make aesthetic choices.[9] This kind of imagination is critical to historical thinking, as all history must be imagined. Museum

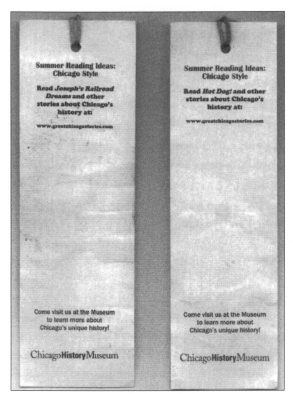 

Bookmark backs, with varied summer reading suggestions. Courtesy of the Chicago History Museum.

Bookmark front. Courtesy of the Chicago History Museum

educators cannot take visitors back in time to see what the 1893 World's Fair was like, but we can encourage visitors to use historical sources to help imagine what the Fair visitors felt, saw, smelled, tasted, heard and touched. Leaving the front of the bookmark mostly blank capitalized on the children's ability to imagine anything.[10]

Finally, to inspire visitors, the bookmarks used new and unusual materials. Since paint, glitter, or other generally messy or wet art supplies were prohibited, we made use of other varied supplies: beads, yarn, 3-D foam stickers and pipe cleaners became staples. Jefferson maintains that this kind of stimulation is critical to having a successful craft: "If the [educator] has on hand some interesting and colorful materials... children will be curious about them and will want to work with them."[11] Foam stickers proved to be so interesting, that they had to be restocked mid-week and continued to be popular into the weekend.

Making it Count — Creating an Effective Learning Environment

Working in a tent is not ideal. Unlike working in a museum — where the environment is carefully monitored — the Millennium Park Tent threw a variety of curveballs. Weather affected attendance. Lack of temperature, light and humidity control prevented us from bringing teaching objects downtown. The informality of the space prevented the volunteers and educators from being able to run structured programs and presented special challenges for creating an effective learning environment.

The first major problem with our space was that it wasn't easily distinguishable as an inside or an outside space. Children rely on this distinction for clues about what kind of play is acceptable. "Indoor" learning environments, like classrooms and museums, should ideally have structured entrance and exit points, areas where noise can be regulated, and activities that encourage quiet, thoughtful play. Details like ceiling height, wall color, lighting and furniture placement should all be considered to create a comfortable space.[12] In contrast, large areas like the Family Fun Tent are more commonly associated with outside spaces, and encourage children to engage in "outdoor" play: running, yelling, using their bodies, and interacting with nature. The tent was simultaneously an indoor and an outdoor space. It was covered so children were out of the elements, but the large floor area, the high ceilings, the lack of controlled light and inability to control volume made it easier to facilitate outdoor play.

In hindsight, we could have been more aggressive with our use of space, to improve effectiveness of the craft area. Event staff provided CHM with picnic tables and bike racks, and they could have been used to partition the area, helping us to better manage the space. This simple tweak would have created the specific entry and exit point needed, made the space smaller, and indicate that our crafts were "inside" activities.

We didn't know it at the time, but craft tables can — and should — be "sticky." People remember large, weird and "cool" things they saw in the museum, and those memories stick with them.[13] Because we had no control over the environment, CHM did not bring sticky objects. Instead, we brought photographs of objects in the CHM collection. Some of them, to our surprise, proved to be extraordinarily sticky. For example, one photograph depicted an 1870's fire engine, as would have been used during the Great Chicago Fire. Almost every person crafting near this photograph asked, "What is that?" initiating a conversation about historic fire trucks and fire prevention. It appears that when used correctly, photographs of sticky objects can be just as sticky as the objects themselves. The unusual photographs inspired visitors to draw what they were seeing on their bookmarks, started conversations about history and tied in the museum. ("Where can I go see that?") More than any other marketing method — exhibit flyers, program listings, free buttons — the sticky photographs helped us achieve all three of our institutional goals.

Relating it Back — Crafting in the Museum

So, given how difficult it is to make a craft work well for a museum, is it really worth it? Yes. Educators can make real connections through artistic and creative enterprises. When a child successfully completes a craft like the "Leave Your Mark on History" bookmark, he is demonstrating that he understands the content thoroughly enough to reinterpret it artistically.

"Creative thinking actually *requires* significant content knowledge, and thinking creatively about a topic helps deepen one's knowledge of that topic."[14] A great deal of children chose to represent the Ferris Wheel, "L" cars and the Willis (formerly Sears) Tower on their bookmarks, showing that they understood what we were asking them to do. Many thought critically about Chicago and history to choose a moment or object that they found personally meaningful.

There were no time limits, but we estimated that each person would probably spend about ten to fifteen minutes crafting. Imaginative play takes time; often more time than children are given in today's society. Visitors were not pressured to move along, as the purpose of a museum is to get visitors to slow down, look at an object and think about it. A craft activity is a perfect complement to this intellectual endeavor. With crafts, we are inviting children (and adults) to sit and think about history. What does it look like? What does it mean to you? Regardless of time and subject matter, if a child is invited into an environment that is thoughtfully constructed, stocked with interesting supplies, and is given clear in-structions that invite broad artistic interpretation, a craft activity can be the perfect way to introduce children to history and the museum.

Notes

1. Anna Reyner, "Arts, Crafts & Creativity in School-Age Child Care & Recreation," Earlychildhood NEWS accessed 8 November 2011; available from http://www.earlychildhoodnews.com/earlychildhood/article_view.aspx?ArticleID=80.

2. Daniel Spock, "Imagination — A Child's Gateway to Engagement with the Past," in *Connecting Kids to History with Museum Exhibitions*, eds. D. Lynn McRainey and John Russick (Walnut Creek, California: Left Coast Press, 2010), 125.

3. Reyner.

4. Sharon Shaffer, "Never Too Young to Connect to History: Cognitive Development and Learning," in *Connecting Kids to History with Museum Exhibitions*, eds. D. Lynn McRainey and John Russick (Walnut Creek, California: Left Coast Press, 2010), 31.

5. Ibid., 41.

6. For a deeper discussion of history, the conversation about fire should have led to the Great Chicago Fire. Once the subject was broached, the educator could bring the conversation full circle, by making a connection to objects one can find at the museum. CHM's Great Chicago Fire collection is one of the premier Fire collections in the world. Melted objects include shooting marbles, carpenter's nails and steel, all salvaged from the 1871 fire.

7. While our focus was primarily on Chicago city history, we needed to check into what other state standards recommend students learn in third, fourth and fifth grade. For example, while fourth graders in Illinois are learning about the structures of the federal and Illinois state governments and about Illinois state history, fourth graders from California are learning to plot points on maps, about the California economy from 1850 Gold Rush to the present and are discussing the life and social interactions of people in California from Pre-Colombian times through the arrival of Spanish missionaries. It would be unfair to ask a fourth grader from California to make meaning of the Great Chicago Fire, the meat-packing industry or the 1893 World's Fair, as she has probably had little to no encounters with the subject matter. "State Standards," *Teachinghistory.org National History Education Clearing House*, accessed 8 November 2011, available from http://teachinghistory.org/teaching-materials/state-standards.

8. With the help of a two-year grant from the National Endowment for the Humanities in 2008, CHM commissioned a series of short fiction pieces based in Chicago history. Working with teachers throughout Chicago, professional authors and oral storytellers, CHM drafted a several short works of historical fiction and posted them online. Each story was supplemented with interactive maps of Chicago, photographs of objects in CHM's collection, audio files and classroom unit extensions, and children are encouraged to learn about different neighborhoods and seminal moments in Chicago history through the eyes of other children. To make the website accessible to a wider range of schools, the stories are divided into two age categories: elementary and high school. The website has won several awards, including the 2008 Gold MUSE Award for Teaching and Outreach from the American Association of Museums Media & Technology Committee, the 2008 Award for Excellence in Published Resources, Student and Teacher Category, from the American Association of Museums Committee on Education, and the 2008 Best of the Web, in the Educational category, from Museums and the Web. "Great Chicago Stories," *The Chicago History Museum*, last updated August 2011, available from http://www.greatchicagostories.com/about/index.php.

9. Blanche Jefferson, *Teaching Art to Children*, 2nd ed. (Boston: Allyn and Bacon Inc, 1963), 126.

10. Spock, 118.

11. Jefferson, 129.

12. Karyn Wellhousen and Ingrid Crowther, *Creating Effective Learning Environments* (Canada: Thomson Learning Inc, 2004), 26.

13. In the blog Museum Audience Insight, the Reach Advisors for community-driven enterprise and museums assert that what makes a museum experience memorable is the "stickiness factor" or the interesting and unusual qualities of an object or exhibit that are most meaningful to a visitor. Using a series of coded memories, the Reach Advisors found that museum collections — objects and artifacts — time and again have proven to be the most

"sticky" part of museum experiences. "Awesome Spaces and Sticky Stuff: Early Childhood Memories of Museums," *Museum Audience Insight* blog, 15 October 2010, available from: http://reachadvisors.typepad.com/museum_audience_insight/2010/10/awesome-spaces-and-sticky-stuff-early-childhood-memories-of-museums.html.

14. John Baer and Tracey Garrett, "Teaching for Creativity in an Era of Content Standards and Accountability," in *Nurturing Creativity in the Classroom*, eds. Ronald A. Beghetto and James C. Kaufman (New York: Cambridge University Press, 2010), 6.

About the Author

Madeline Karp worked as an intern with the Chicago History Museum during the summer of 2011, where she primarily focused on creating crafts for the Millennium Park Family Fun Festival. She has an interest in education through role-playing and hands-on activity, and has worked with American Revolutionary War re-enactors to study the value of imagination and self-immersion in historical education. Madeline is a recent graduate of Tufts University's Museum Education program.

It's All Fun and Games in *Tiny's Diner*

Preschool Programming in Unusual Exhibit Spaces

Nora Moynihan and Betsy Diamant-Cohen

Abstract   This article describes the challenges of creating educational programs for guided groups that teach about healthy eating, strengthen school readiness skills, include picture book read-alouds, and keep young children engaged, while in exhibit spaces that were meant for free play.

Kids enter the diner wanting to play;
How do you teach nutrition this way?
When a school system pays
To enhance children's days
They expect EDUCATION in informal ways.

Welcome to Port Discovery's *Tiny's Diner* where children can be seen doing the chicken dance or putting pickles on their heads. What do these activities have to do with promoting nutrition through early literacy activities? Educators know that young children learn through play,[1] which can include using drama, games, movement, imagination, and music.[2] They respond to humor and enjoy novelty.[3] Add a book as the focal point, and you have Port Discovery's recipe for a healthy program.[4]

When schools choose guided tours instead of opting for free-flow visits, the museum is obligated to provide a formal program worth the extra expense. Creating programs for free-flow areas, such as a diner, can be challenging, however. As soon as children enter enticing exhibit spaces, they immediately want to play. The education department at Port Discovery has worked hard to create a formula that combines formal programming with free play in a fun atmosphere where children are engaged and teachers understand the educational value of the program. We aim to impart the message of healthy eating and nutrition while keeping the children's attention and providing a fun experience.[5]

Entering school ready to learn sets a framework for a child's success both in school and in life.[6] Children who enter school "ready to learn" are more likely to graduate from high school, hold down a job, have higher earnings, and commit fewer crimes.[7] There is also a significant economic benefit to society when children enter school ready to learn.[8] This year, only 65% of Baltimore City children entered kindergarten fully ready to learn.[9] Port Discovery strives to raise these numbers though interactive exhibits and programs,[10] recognizing that positive, playful experiences in the earliest years nurture a child's ability to learn.[11] Thus, the Education Department intentionally creates programs that help pre-schoolers build language and literacy skills.[12] Since obesity is a huge problem in the United States today, diner programs also are designed to teach children about healthy eating.[13]

Through play, young visitors build knowledge of the world around them and their place in it.[14] Creative play sparks the imagination, encouraging children to see beyond the known, practice teamwork, follow directions, and exercise problem solving skills.[15] By offering programs created for the under-five crowd, Port Discovery is addressing the needs of early learners, an essential aspect of children's museums.[16]

Port Discovery's Strategies for Creating Healthy Food-related Programs

Over time, we've created a strategy for developing school programs in the diner. We change them frequently to keep them fresh. We always start by choosing the read-aloud book. All of our programs meet the follow criteria:

1. Support the common core standards.[17]

2. Be captivating for the audience.

3. Be short in duration.

4. Promote nutrition.

5. Utilize the exhibit space in a unique way.

6. Include elements that educators will consider valuable.

7. Be interactive.

8. Have an element of humor.

9. Include a literacy component (read-aloud book).

10. Activate more than one of the intelligences.[18]

Once a picture book has been chosen for a diner program, the planning begins. We look for fun activities that support the healthy eating theme while also complementing the book being read aloud.[19] Brainstorming together, modifying games we played as children, looking through books, and searching on the Internet are ways we find theme-related activities that fit into a programming area of *Tiny's Diner*.[20]

We send a copy of the proposed program to the Early Childhood "Ed-Ventures Team," an advisory group of educators consisting of two preschool teachers, one college professor, one early literacy professional, two children's librarians, one teacher, one nutritionist, and one museum professional for comments. Once feedback has been received and integrated (or not!) into the program, the early childhood specialist writes a description for our Special Programs Guide. The guide is posted on the museum's website and distributed to teachers in different venues such as conferences and teacher trainings. The guide reminds teachers to ask if programs are available in *Tiny's Diner* when booking visits; the group sales team follows up by mentioning the programs while booking school visits over the phone.

Guided preschool and early elementary classes at Port Discovery are booked for 45-minute sessions in each museum space. During the time that a class is scheduled for a program in *Tiny's Diner*, the doors to the exhibit are closed and the program begins. The first fifteen or twenty minutes are spent presenting the formal program; the remainder of the time is given to free play. *Tiny's Diner* is a

Families play together in *Tiny's Diner*.

replica of an actual diner which offers children a place to increase their ability both to listen and speak through dramatic play.[21] Early learners have opportunities to socialize, use their imaginations, and practice creative thinking and problem solving as they experiment with real life situations. [22]

Since the first moments set the tone for the rest of the session, programs generally start with a healthy dose of humor that grabs the children's attention. One program, "Who Would Eat a Shoe?" begins when a museum program associate wearing a chef's hat welcomes everyone into the diner and displays three plates, each one covered by a cloth. The chef whips the cover off the first plate to reveal.... YARN! On the second plate is.... A tin can! And on the third plate is.... AN OLD SHOE! Who would want to eat those things? Perhaps a goat!

This introduction leads into reading aloud the picture book *Gregory, the Terrible Eater* by Mitchell Sharmat.[23] When the story is finished, the program leader conducts a brief discussion about nutritious food. Children then examine pictures of all the foods and objects eaten by Gregory in the story. They take turns coming up to a flannel board with a line down the middle and place their picture either on the side labeled "people food" or on the other side labeled "goat food." When the program finishes, children are invited to create some nutritious dishes in the diner as they begin free play. This is typical of the diner programs at Port Discovery.

Music plays an important part in the fun and educational activities that we've devised. Dancing peas (laminated green construction paper circles), inspired by *Eat Your Peas, Louise* by Pegeen Snow, invite children to sing and dance the "Hokey Pea-okey" ("You put your pea in, you take your pea out, you put your pea in, and you shake it all about") and "Head, Shoulders, PEAS and Toes."[24] Program associates have the option of presenting a Kamishibai Theatre show to a silly song which we discovered on YouTube, "I Got a Pea" by Bryant Oden.[25] In addition to the book and the funny activities, children look at photographs of peas growing in gardens, pea pods, children shelling peas, and pea soup. To help them get started with free play, we tell them that the special of the day in *Tiny's Diner* is pea soup.

A current program features the book. *Two Eggs, Please*, by Sarah Weeks.[26] While giving the message that people are both different and the same, this book also lists a number of ways that eggs can be prepared. After the story is read, children pretend to be different kinds of eggs. Have you ever seen a child trying to be a sunny side up egg? What about a poached egg? Or hard-boiled? Children are able to exercise their imaginations and their bodies during this movement activity. And, if they have difficulty coming up with ideas, program associates are ready to prompt them, using teaching ideas suggested in the lesson plan. This program ends with "The Chicken Dance" and children are then invited to create some healthy breakfasts as they begin their free-play.

Through informal conversations, program associate feedback, and written teacher surveys, it is clear that the formal program enhances the following free play.[27] Response from other educators has been positive. Dr. Lisa Parker Eason, principal of the Dr. Rayner Browne Academy in Baltimore, appreciates the connection between the common core standards and the programs.[28] Susan Hahn, Parent Services Representative from Baltimore County Public Schools, considers the diner programs to be "a great day of learning."[29]

"Combining nutrition, literacy, learning, and play is very important at the preschool and elementary school age," says Lyssa Balick, a nutritionist for McCormick and Company, Inc. who presents "Cook and Tell" programs in *Tiny's Diner* along with Port Discovery staff.[30] She continued,

> We enjoy this approach when we partner with Port Discovery to show how kids can use spices and herbs to flavor healthy foods. Children in a group setting have different learning styles and backgrounds. But there is something they all have in common: all kids like to play. Port Discovery makes healthy food programs interactive and fun for everyone. Port Discovery teaches the important nutritional messages that healthy food can taste good and that eating nutritious food is easy and something everyone can do. In *Tiny's Diner* programs, children don't just hear books being read aloud; they also play with the words — using music and cooking and movement and fun. It is the perfect learning environment.[31]

Because the programs in *Tiny's Diner* captivate children's hearts and minds, children are able to focus on the book and activities before free play begins. Teachers see the educational value of the programs and program associates are able to impart the message about nutrition in a relaxed, non-didactic way. Everybody wins! The most important part of these programs, however, is the health benefit of fun and laughter which is shared by all.[32]

Notes

1. Kathy Hirsh-Pasek, Roberta M. Golinkoff, and Diane E. Eyer, *Einstein Never Used Flash Cards: How Our Children Really Learn--and Why They Need to Play More and Memorize Less* (Emmaus, Pa: Rodale, 2003); David Elkind, *The Power of Play: Learning What Comes Naturally* (Cambridge, MA: Da Capo Press, 2007).

2. Frances M. Carlson, *Big Body Play: Why Boisterous, Vigorous, and Very Physical Play is Essential to Children's Development and Learning* (Washington, DC: National Association for the Education of Young Children, 2011); Bergen, Doris, "The Role of Pretend Play in Children's Cognitive Development." *Early Childhood Research and Practice* 4, no. 1, (2002) http://ecrp.uiuc.edu/v4n1/bergen.html; Barbara Cass-Beggs, *Your Child Needs Music* (Mississauga, Ontario: The Frederick Harris Music Co., 1986); Ann Barlin and Paul Barlin (authors), and David Alexander (photographer), *The Art of Learning Through Movement* (Los Angeles: Ward Ritchie, 1973); Betsy Diamant-Cohen, Tess Prendergast, Christy Estrovitz, Carrie Banks, and Kim Van der Veen, "We Play Here! Bringing the Power of Play into Children's Libraries" *Children and Libraries* 10, no.1 (2012): 3–9; Frank Forencich, *Exuberant Animal: The Power of Health, Play, and Joyful Movement.* (Bloomington, IN: AuthorHouse, 2006).

3. D'Arcy Lyness, "Encouraging Your Child's Sense of Humor." KidsHealth — the Web's most visited site about children's health. The Nemours Foundation. (2012). http://kidshealth.org/parent/growth/learning/child_humor.html.

4. Mem Fox, Reading Magic: *Why Reading Aloud to our Children Will Change Their Lives Forever* (New York: Harcourt, 2001); Zigler, Edward, Dorothy G. Singer, and Sandra J. Bishop-Josef, eds., *Children's Play; The Roots of Reading.* (Washington, DC: Zero to Three Press, 2004); Susan B. Neuman, "Books Make A Difference: A Study of Access to Literacy" *Reading Research Quarterly* 34, no. 3 (1999): 286–311.

5. Connie Liakos Evers, *How to Teach Nutrition to Kids* (Portland, OR: 24 Carrot Press, 2006) is a useful resource.

6. National Research Council, *Eager to Learn: Educating our Preschoolers* (Washington DC: National Academy Press, 2001).

7. Highscope Educational Reseach Foundation, *HighScope Perry Preschool Study: Lifetime Effects: The HighScope Perry Preschool Study Through Age 40* (2005). http://www.highscope.org/content.asp?contentid=219.

8. James J. Heckman, in *Schools, Skills and Synapses* (Bonn, Germany: Institute for the Study of Labor, 2008), uses mathematical formulas to explain the economic benefit for investing in early childhood education. Savings due to lower rates of incarceration are significant. "Heckman: The Economics of Human Potential." http://www.heckmanequation.org/content/resource/school-skills-synapses (accessed June 2012).

9. The Annie E. Casey Foundation, "Data by State/Maryland/Ready for Kindergarten-Average of Language and Literacy and Mathematical Thinking (Percent) 2011-2012." Kids Count Data Center (2012). http://datacenter.kidscount.org/data/bystate/Rankings.aspx?state=MD&ind=4502 (accessed May 2012).

10. Although this is a big increase from 2008 when only 50% of children entered school fully ready to learn, Port Discovery would like to see percentage rise much more. The Annie E. Casey Foundation, "Data by State/Maryland/Ready for Kindergarten-Average of Language and Literacy and Mathematical Thinking (Percent) 2007-2008." Kids Count Data Center,(2012). http://datacenter.kidscount.org/data/bystate/Rankings.aspx?state=MD&loct=5&by=a&order=a&ind=4502&dtm=10283&tf=118 (accessed June 2012).

11. Stuart L. Brown and Christopher C. Vaughn, *Play: How it Shapes the Brain, Opens the Imagination, and Invigorates the Soul* (New York: Avery, 2009).

12. Language and literacy skills are strengthened by providing positive experiences with books, a model of book reading behavior, and exposure to new vocabulary words. R. B McCathren and J. H. Allor, "Using Storybooks with Preschool Children: Enhancing Language and Emergent Literacy" *Young Exceptional Children* 5, no. 4 (2002): 3–10; Roskos, Kathleen, and Susan Neuman. "Play as an Opportunity for Literacy. In *Multiple Perspectives on Play in Early Childhood*, edited by Olivia N. Saracho and Bernard Spodek (Albany, NY: State University of New York Press, 1998): 100–115.

13. American Academy of Child & Adolescent Psychiatry, "Obesity in Children and Teens," *Facts for Families*, March (2011). http://www.aacap.org/cs/root/facts_for_families/obesity_in_children_and_teens (accessed May 2012).
14. Gyroscope Inc., "Standards of Excellence in Early Learning: A Model for Chicago Children's Museum" (2005). Standards of Excellence. www.childrensmuseums.org/docs/StandardsofExcellence.pdf (accessed May 20 2012); Kathy Hirsh-Pasek and Roberta M. Golinkoff, "Play = Learning: How Play Motivates and Enhances Children's Cognitive and Social-Emotional Growth" (2011). http://udel.edu/~roberta/play/index.html; Cosby S. Rogers, and Janet K. Sawyers, *Play in the Lives of Children* (Washington, DC: National Association for the Education of Young Children, 1988).
15. Vivian Gussin Paley, *A Child's Work: The Importance of Fantasy Play* (Chicago: University of Chicago Press, 2004).
16. Betsy Bowers, "A Look at Early Childhood Programming in Museums," *Journal of Museum Education* 37, no.1 (2012): 39–41.
17. The common core standards are outlines and lists that spell out what students of varying ages are expected to learn, based on age-appropriate development. They are meant to serve as a guide for teachers and parents by explaining in detail the standards of success in school; the adults are then expected to use these standards to help their children. Currently, 45 states and three US territories have formally adopted the standards. Common Core Standard Initiatives, "Common Core State Standards Initiative," (2012). http://www.corestandards.org/.
18. Howard Gardner, *Intelligence Reframed: Multiple Intelligences for the 21st Century* (New York: Basic Books, 2000).
19. There are many books with picture book programming ideas related to food including Jan Irving and Robin Currie's book, *Mudlicious: Stories and Activities Featuring Food for Preschool Children* (Littleton, CO: Libraries Unlimited, 1986); Wendy Camilla Blackwell, *Family Literacy Projects on a Budget: A Trainers' Toolkit* (Washington: National Children's Museum, 2009); Toni W. Linder, *Read, Play, and Learn! Storybook Activities for Young Children* (Baltimore: Paul H. Brookes, 1999); Pat Murphy, Ellen Macaulay, Jason Gorski, and the staff of the Exploratorium, *Exploratopia* (New York: Little Brown and Company, 2006); Sue McCleaf Nespeca and Joan B. Reeve, *Picture Books Plus: 100 Extension Activities in Art, Drama, Music, Math, and Science* (Chicago: ALA Editions. 2003); Ontario Science Center, *Foodworks: Over 100 Science Activities and Fascinating Facts that Explore the Magic of Food* (Reading, Mass: Addison-Wesley, 1987).
20. *Tiny's Diner* is 672 square feet; the programming area is approximately 11′ × 26′.
21. Mary Renck Jalongo, *Learning to Listen, Listening to Learn* (Washington, DC: National Association for the Education of Young Children, 2008).
22. Russ, S. W., "Play, Creativity, and Adaptive Functioning: Implications for Play Interventions" *Journal of Clinical Child Psychology* 27, no. 4 (1998): 469–80.
23. Mitchell Sharmat (author), Jose Aruego (illustrator), and Ariane Dewey (illustrator), *Gregory, the Terrible Eater* (New York: Four Winds Press, 1980).
24. Pegeen Snow (author), Mike Venezia (illustrator), *Eat Your Peas, Louise* (Chicago: Children's Press, 1991).
25. Kamishibai Theatre is an old form of Japanese story-telling that involves showing illustrations on paper cards one at a time and reading a script on the back of the last card while sliding the first one across. More information about Kamishibai can be found at http://www.kamishibai.com/educators/readers_theatre.html. Permission to use the song was obtained from Bryant Oden. "I Got A Pea" is located on *Songdrops: 30 Songs for Kids* [S.I.]: (CD Baby, 2009), and can be accessed from: http://www.youtube.com/watch?v=1Q6DdTcqGy8.

26. Sarah Weeks (author) and Betsy Lewin (illustrator), *Two Eggs, Please* (New York: Aladdin Paperbacks, 2003).
27. Based on Port Discovery teacher exit surveys from Sept. 2011–May 2012.
28. Excerpt from Dr. Lisa Parker Eason's email to Nora Moynihan on May 22, 2012.
29. Excerpt from Susan Hahn's email to Nora Moynihan on June 2, 2012.
30. Excerpt from Lyssa Balick's email to Betsy Diamant-Cohen on May 23, 2012.
31. Ibid.
32. B. L. Fredrickson, "Cultivating Positive Emotions to Optimize Health and Well-Being," *Prevention and Treatment* 3, no. 1 (2000). http://www.rickhanson.net/wp-content/files/papers/CultPosEmot.pdf; Silvia H. Cardoso, "Our Ancient Laughing Brain," *Cerebrum* 2, no. 4 (2000): 15–30.

About the Authors

Nora Moynihan, Director of Education and Community Enrichment at Port Discovery, The Children's Museum in Baltimore, has a BS and MS in Early Childhood Education from Southern Connecticut State University with Post-graduate work from the University of Syracuse and Bank Street College. Her experience ranges from Head Start Administration to an adjunct professorship in Early Childhood at Florida Community College.

Dr. Betsy Diamant-Cohen, creator of the award-winning Mother Goose on the Loose® early literacy program (www.mothergooseontheloose.com) and author of several books, is Port Discovery's Early Childhood Specialist. She holds a Master's Degree in Library Science and a Doctorate in Communications Design. In addition to being a librarian, teacher, museum professional, storyteller, and educator, Betsy consults on children's programming and presents training workshops throughout the United States.

Exploring the Educational Future

Elizabeth E. Merritt

Abstract   Futures studies uses scenarios—stories of the future—to explore how trends and events shaping our world may play out in future decades. This article features a short scenario set in California in 2037, depicting twelve-year-old Moya and her brother Inart, whose "fenced community" has opted for a system of self-directed, online learning to educate its children. This scenario, and the accompanying discussion questions, can be used to guide a conversation about how museums could fit into the future landscape of learning.

The role of futures studies is to help us notice the trends and events that may disrupt our expected path into the future and imagine the variety of potential futures that we face. Forecasting suggests we are on the cusp of transformative change in America's educational system: Indicators include rising levels of dissatisfaction with traditional schools and increasing experimentation with alternative systems (e.g., home schooling and charter schools). There is a growing consensus that traditional classrooms may not be the best environment to foster key 21st-century skills such as collaboration, creativity and critical thinking. The Internet has opened up a wealth of new resources to learners, while schools embrace online learning as a cost-saving measure. Students entering higher education today struggle to calculate the economic value of a degree with the cost (and debt) that entails, which in turn creates a market for alternate forms of credentialing.

These educational forces play out in a century shaped by larger demographic, economic, political and social forces. We are nurturing the first generation of "digital natives," children as comfortable navigating the online realm as the streets of their neighborhood. We are increasingly concerned about the consequences of the rapid increase in the huge divide between wealthy and average

Journal of Museum Education, Volume 37, Number 3, Fall 2012, pp. 99–106.

Americans. The obesity crisis is making alarming strides — one third of children born in 2000 or later are projected to develop diabetes in their lifetime. Rising fuel prices will at some point radically increase the cost of travel and shipping, driving localization of manufacturing, agriculture and a reduction in commuting. States are already scrambling to cut budgets in the wake of the mortgage loan crisis, including deep cuts to basic public goods — education, police, sanitation — raising the possibility that we might reach a tipping point where these services are privatized altogether.

If forecasting is the science of spotting and cataloging these trends, scenario creation is the art of bringing them to life. Scenarios are little "stories of the future" that help us imagine the world we might live in twenty-five, fifty or one hundred years from now. We can, for example, look at the trends summarized above and ask, what might education look like in the U.S. in a quarter century? What role might museums play in that educational future? In that spirit, I offer one such story as food for thought:

A Learning Day 2037

Moya sighed in frustration, tearing off her auggles and rubbing her temples, which ached from the ill-fitting headset. When working properly, the frames projected digital data onto her cornea, seamlessly overlaying digital images from the Museo's archive with the community timeline she was creating. This set, though, was a hand-me-down from her cousin, and when Renata was Moya's age, she was a lot smaller, with the delicate bones and fine facial structure shared by her mother and Moya's mom. Moya was acutely aware she had inherited the broad cheeks and wide temples of her father's Meximericano family.

The auggles were inferior to implants, but no one was going to waste community funds on bioaugments for a twelve year old, however bright and talented. Moya knew she should be grateful for any integrated AR access — she'd earned this privilege by having her exhibit design chosen by community consensus for installation in Museo, the community museum. Now she was counting on the project to earn enough credits in research, history and fabrication to qualify her for a digital apprenticeship at one of the "real" museums on the outside. With the imprint of the Oakland Museum of California, the Tech Museum of Innovation, or maybe even the SI on her digital badge resumé, she'd be well on her way to professional track training.

Any child with sense, growing up in Oyamina, aimed for professional or paraprofessional training. Working in remote medical monitoring or prototype fabrication, or as a virtual health/wellness coach, beat the heck out of toiling in the Community Farm, even though the Farm was the foundation of the Community's stability and independence. Bill Allen had demonstrated, back in the '10s, that three acres could feed 10,000 people. With only three thousand-some residents inside its fortified fence, Oyamina raised enough extra food — fruit and vegetables, fish, rabbits, chickens and eggs — to trade for hard cash Outside. The digital currency generated by the professional track workers was fine for some things, but it took hard cash to pay the spiraling water fees (legal and under the table) that made Oyamina possible.

Young women, of course, had the option of becoming Wombs, but even though Renata bragged on the perks of that job — the first-rate health care, access to ample food even in hard times, no field work — Moya had no intention of renting her body out that way.

In her secret heart of hearts, she aimed high. She wanted to be chosen as an Innovator — one of the select talents who trawled the cloud looking for challenges to answer. There was, of course, the prospect of huge payoffs for Innovators who won one of the competitions posted by the major corporations. But more than that, Moya coveted the access Innovators had to the Community's best technology and support. When cousin Mano teased her about her cheekbones, straggly hair or awkward height, she comforted herself by imagining the pimply young technologist being assigned to prototype one of her creations. *That* would put him in his place.

"Come back here, you little demon!" Shrieks from outside disrupted Moya's daydreams a few seconds before Inart came tearing into the room, clutching a ripe peach. "Hide me!" he panted, throwing himself under the desk. Moya ran to the window in time to see their father striding past on the sidewalk. Rand was a big man, and with his belt already coiled around his hand he was a fearsome sight, indeed.

Moya spared a moment of sympathy for Inart, even if he was an idiot to think that Rand, in his role as Farm Manager, could afford to look the other way when Inart and his crew of nine-year-old hellions stole from the fields. That kind of "foraging" was one of the few crimes that could get an adult thrown out of the Community, and once outside Oyamina's fortifications, the options were pretty grim. Moya had seen the vids of gangs roaming the streets of unfenced cities and towns. With no private security forces or maintenance staff, these "Open Street" neighborhoods were dirty, dangerous and almost impossible to work your way out of. Moya worried that this was exactly where Inart was going to end up. Sure, there were plenty of academically lazy kids who, as they grew older, dropped out of the

Community's self-directed learning program. Rand depended on it—he was happy to scoop them up, at fifteen or sixteen, and apprentice them to the orchards or the fish tanks. But Inart didn't even have the discipline for that—Moya worried he was going to jump the fence one day and end up as unskilled labor conscripted into a company town (at best), or recruited into a gang that might in the short run be exciting and lucrative—but that was liable to be a very short run indeed.

"Inart!" She made her voice sharp, even as she laughed inside at the sight of peach juice dripping down his face. "You're crazy, boy! You think Poppa won't catch up to you at dinner? You think he'll forget by then?! He's gonna be waiting inside the dining hall door with his belt ready." Inart rolled out from underneath the desk, dusting himself off and reaching into his shirt to present Moya with a second, perfectly ripe peach, slightly bruised from his flight. "Yah, but Imma will be there; she won't let him wale on me too hard." He bit into his peach, the juice rolling down his chin. "It was worth it—all this fruit and what do we get at dinner? Rice! And catfish. I'm sick of catfish. I'm sick of rice, too. What's the good of Poppa being Farm Manager if he can't get us some of the good stuff?"

Moya contemplated the peach for a moment before shrugging and taking a bite. Pragmatically, someone had to destroy the evidence, and Inart would eat it if she didn't. She found it a point of pride that their poppa was so straight up that he wouldn't cheat, wouldn't take the bribes that outsiders regularly offered to bypass the Community's formal distribution contracts. But she did share Inart's regret about the peaches.

She wasn't about to let her brother off the hook, though. "Why aren't you working on your math? You're way behind on that, I know." Inart hadn't even passed the third level, when most of the kids he hung with, even some littler ones, were on to the fourth or fifth level in math. Inart rolled his eyes. "It's booooooooring," he lamented, throwing out his arms, collapsing over Moya's desk and snoring loudly to dramatize just how soporific he found numbers. "Tough. You can use the work station over there to access Khan Plus—or bring up one of the games programs—you choose! But you're going level up at least once by the end of the afternoon, or I won't help you out with Poppa tonight," Moya retorted.

Inart stopped snoring and lay still for a minute, considering his options. The online tutorials weren't too bad—at least they didn't make him feel dumb (only frustrated), and some of the games were cool. His favorite let you cut deals for water rights and trade commodities (legal or not) to maximize your profit. Even at nine, Inart was all about profit, if only he didn't have to work too hard for it. He flipped over and shoved himself off the desk into Moya's chair, rolling across the room to the monitor. "Okay, deal. I level up one and you plead my case with

Pops." He scanned in, accessed the MarketForce program, and soon was totally engrossed in calculating how much fish feed to buy, and at what price, to maximize a catfish crop from the animated aquiculture tanks.

Moya sighed and, flipping the auggles back in place, flicked her eyes to resume the project. The most frustrating thing was, Inart wasn't dumb. He was just never going to study if no one sat him down and forced him. Some other fenced communities had opted for old-fashioned schools with grades, real, in-person teachers and mandatory testing. She was a little hazy on what they did, exactly, with kids who failed the tests, but at least they provided some structure. Oyamina, for better or worse, had opted for self-directed learning. Mind you, the Community devoted considerable resources to the system — high-speed data connections, ample cloud storage, subscriptions to high-quality online programs, even fees for individual virtual tutors for the kids who needed extra help (and were willing to work) or had maxed out the potential of the other resources.

Moya was one of the latter. She'd blazed through the Khan Plus programs in math, history and economics by the time she was Inart's age. Her Personal Learning Mentor had smiled and pointed her to more advanced material, even quietly unlocking some of the proscribed sites that weren't on the list of Community-approved resources. That's when she began secretly visiting art museums — great digital repositories of stuff like she'd never seen before. Math, economics, engineering, biology, agriculture — these were practical subjects, training learners to staff the Community's core tracks. Art was frivolous, a waste of time and resources. Moya didn't even tell her imma she'd been wandering through the virtual galleries of the Met, the Hermitage, the Uffizi. Leiya loved her daughter and indulged her to a certain extent, but she was also ruthlessly practical. She'd worked hard to qualify as virtual health coach, and she wanted Moya to do better for herself. Studying art wasn't going to boost her into a higher track in the Community.

So Moya usually channeled her creative energy into fabrication, booking time on the second-rank 3-D digital printers in the maker lab, occasionally coaxing Mano into giving her access to one of the first-rank machines when she had a particularly precise design to prototype. That's why the Museo project was so exciting — winning the design competition meant she had access to the museum's digital collections, even its archive of rare physical documents. She'd spent one long afternoon engrossed in reading actual postcards (with stamps!) from Oyamina's founder to his wife-to-be. There were even photographic prints of the community before it was fenced — shots from the twentieth century showing clapboard houses, winding streets, people driving cars (!) through what was now a mixture of vertical farms, office buildings, dormitories, solar arrays and water storage towers linked by pedestrian and bike trails, with occasional access roads for delivery vehicles.

Moya was inventorying and geomapping elements — single family homes, businesses, even a few trees — that predated Oyamina's fence, and creating an AR app that would let people stroll through the Community, seeing it as it had been twenty, thirty or fifty years ago. In a small exhibit hall in the Museo itself she was staging a display of physical artifacts culled from the collections and borrowed from friends and neighbors that illustrated the Community's history: a shovel aunt Tami had inherited from her grandpa Luke, the Farm's first manager and Rand's mentor; a ceremonial copy of the "Articles of Incorporation" that had been filed with the State of California, on thick, cotton-rag paper with an impressive seal and ribbon; a partially burnt book (a physical one, with a hard cover and paper pages, still smelling of smoke) salvaged from the Great Raid of 2028 — the first time the Community had to beat back an organized group of pillagers.

"Done!" Inart kicked back from his workstation, spinning the chair across the room to bump against Moya's stool. "Leveled up! I rock too hard for words." He sprang up and did a victory dance, copying some of the moves from the latest sports vids. He looked ridiculous, but cute. "Come on! Turn that dang thing off and come shoot hoops with me before dinner. You need to log some PE time anyway or Imma's going to be on your tail while Pops goes for mine." It was true — Leiya took her role as health coach very seriously. Oyamina couldn't afford the health care costs for diabetes, heart disease, neuropathy and asthma that came with the high obesity rate plaguing many other communities. Not to mention the lost value of labor, when people were unable to work. So in addition to her virtual clients, Moya's mother supervised the health, fitness and nutrition program for the Community's kids.

"In a minute," Moya said, conceding his logic. "You go find a ball, and I'll be down soon. I got one more thing to do." As Inart clattered down the stairs, she flicked her eyes again, bringing up her digital resumé and her half-completed application for the museum apprenticeship. She scanned the documents, noting the prerequisites she hadn't yet filled in, mentally plotting what assignments she could choose to bridge the gap. "I'm gonna make it," she muttered. "I'm gonna level my way up and then . . . watch out." With a sharp nod she saved and closed the files, shut down the system and carefully nested the annoying auggles into their case before trailing after her brother into the warm California dusk.

Exploring Implications

Moya's world isn't the most likely future for the U.S., but it is one of many entirely plausible futures. Exploring these possible futures helps us prepare for circumstances museums will contend with in coming decades. By challenging assumptions about education (universal; free; public; taking place in schools; directed by teachers), it makes us realize how very different things could be. This, in turn, can shape our thinking about how we recruit and train museum educators and plan for our museums.

I encourage you to use this scenario as a jumping-off point to explore the implications of these trends for your own organization and for the field. Points for discussion include:

- What do you see happening in the world around you that might point in the direction of this future or one like it?

- Do you see this as a preferred future, or one to be avoided? If the latter, what steps do you think society could take now to head it off?

- What is the educational landscape of your community (in school and out)? What are the needs, the gaps and the challenges, and what is the most important role your museum can fill in this environment?

- How will your museum find and serve learners who could benefit most from your resources?

- In a world of limited resources, will your museum focus on providing virtual or in-person learning experiences?

- How might your museum contribute to a system of credentialing (e.g., digital badges) for learners of any age, including those who have opted out of the traditional system?

Using A Learning Day 2037 to catalyze discussion around these and other questions in your own institution can expand your thinking about the future you may face, what educational future you want for the U.S. and how your museum can help guide us to that future, one step at a time.

Suggested Reading

American Association of Museums. 2012. *TrendsWatch 2012: Museums and the Pulse of the Future.* This report profiles several trends relevant to the scenario presented above, including the influence of augmented reality and Internet-connected devices on museums, as well as making the case that we may face transformative changes in the U.S. educational system in the near future. Download from www.futureofmuseums.org.

American Association of Museums and the California Association of Museums. 2010. *Tomorrow in the Golden State: Museums and the Future of California*. This report features a scenario depicting the spread of gated communities and hyper-local community museums. Download from www. futureofmuseums.org.

Butler, Octavia. 1993. *Parable of the Sower*. New York: Four Walls Eight Windows. Dystopian futurist novel depicting California in 2025. Many of the background elements in *A Learning Day 2037* are adapted from this novel.

KnowledgeWorks Foundation and the Institute for the Future. 2008. *2020 Forecast: Creating the Future of Learning*. Download from www.kwfdn.org.

Other Resources

Archived interviews with practitioners from many fields on the future of education at www.futureofeducation.com.

Videos (assorted) depicting scenarios from the future of education, on the Future of Education channel on YouTube at www.youtube.com/user/futureofed.

About the Author

Elizabeth Merritt is the Founding Director, Center for the Future of Museums at the American Association of Museums. Her books include National Standards and Best Practices for U.S. Museums and the AAM Guide to Collections Planning. She blogs for CFM at futureofmuseums.blogspot.com and tweets as @futureofmuseums.

All Together Now

Museums and Online Collaborative Learning

By William B. Crow and Herminia Wei-Hsin Din

Reviewed by Jayne Gordon

William Crow and Herminia Wei-Hsin Din are no strangers to the field of online learning. Crow is responsible for K–12 programming at the Metropolitan Museum of Art in New York City, and teaches both Museum Studies courses at Johns Hopkins and Media Studies courses at The New School. Din is Associate Professor of Art Education at the University of Alaska Anchorage and specializes in distance and online learning for museums. She was co-editor of *The Digital Museum: A Think Guide*, published by the AAM Press in 2007. Crow and Din together wrote *Unbound by Place or Time: Museums and Online Learning*, also published by AAM in 2009.

Now this expert team investigates the implications of online learning for collaboration and collaboration for online learning. It's that *combination* that gives this book a unique place on our museum education bookshelf. Crow and Din state right from the beginning that "...we have focused our attention on the concepts and strategies involved in online collaboration, rather than giving focus to the technological tools themselves." They remind us that those tools change constantly — "on an almost daily basis."[1]

What does it mean for collaboration when the boundaries of space and time are erased? How does that change the way we think about and work on collaboration? How does the online dimension expand and change the nature of participation by both the developers and intended audiences during the continuum of an educational project?

Journal of Museum Education, Volume 35, Number 3, Fall 2012, pp. 107–112.

The challenge with a book like this is to keep it from being too abstract, too nebulous, too "show and tell-y." Who, in this day and age, does NOT believe in the exponential power of online tools to bring people together? Who does NOT believe in the value of collaboration? What insights could we possibly have on either of those subjects that would give us a new, refreshing perspective on possibilities that we couldn't have imagined a few short years ago?

Crow and Din solve this problem by interspersing the more philosophical and pedagogical chapters with case studies that exemplify ideas and strategies put into practice. An introductory chapter on "Shared Spaces" is followed by an article by Michael Edson, Director of Web and New Media Strategy for the Smithsonian, describing the building of the Smithsonian Commons. This new initiative involves shared digital space with dozens of museums and research centers working together, over 150 affiliate museums, and millions of collection items, 6.4 million of which have been digitized. Edson thinks of a "commons" as "a kind of organized workshop where the raw materials of knowledge and innovation can be found and assembled into new things."[2] So what do we do with or "in" that shared space, that workshop, that "commons?" *All Together Now* provides some helpful context for subsequent chapters with a discussion of historical foundations and theoretical frameworks for online collaboration, as well as the forms it can take. The significance of this new approach for our museum world is summed up by the authors: "…online collaborative learning can be a way for institutions to shift from being teaching institutions to learning institutions."[3]

Exactly how does that transformation happen? A sample from two venerable San Francisco museums — one art, one science — demonstrates how the online component of a teacher workshop can lengthen the life and extend the community of learners beyond the time, place, and number of original participants. In this case, curricular and professional development resources for teachers fostered a continued integration of activities with an impact that went far beyond the original face-to-face sessions.

The climate essential to any kind of collaborative learning is well documented in this book, as is the culture that emerges from the inception of planning through the implementation of those plans, and then on through the evaluation of the process and the continued use of what has been created. "The very essence of collaboration rests on the premises of shared responsibility and collective accountability."[4] One case study of a leadership symposium of 13 sites located in San Diego's Balboa Park illustrates how a combination of on-site and online — *blended* — learning can make the most effective use of physical and virtual gatherings. But we are still left with the question about how collaboration online is a fundamentally distinctive experience, apart from the collaborations most museums have been practicing for decades. What's truly *different* this time around?

At this point, *All Together Now* becomes more narrowly and necessarily focused on the ingredients that comprise the unique course of *online* collaboration. Material on the stages of e-group development and the ways that e-teachers effectively facilitate the forging of a common group identity are good touchstones for understanding the operation of these "communities of practice."[5]

With any community of practice bringing together diverse institutions across state and even national boundaries, there are immense challenges that need to be met so that the programs don't become cobbled-together, artificially-forced, fragmented hybrids. A case study of the "I Dig Science" program, which partnered a Brooklyn-based organization focused on international issues (Global Kids) with the Field Museum in Chicago, examines the importance of sticking to mission for each of the partners. The other case study in this part of the book highlights the role that a core subject or theme plays in ensuring that the members of the online community inhabit common ground — in this instance, teachers and museum educators working together around an integrated arts curriculum based on a travelling Georgia O'Keeffe exhibition. Her "... artworks became a shared language that unified all of the participants" and "served as a type of 'control'..." for the group.[6]

One of the most intriguing questions to come out of the O'Keeffe study is whether in-person and online communities can exist within the same project. The project evaluator Jeanne Ancelet from Audience Focus is quoted as saying, "The activities and intimate settings experienced during the three [in-person] forums certainly overshadowed and, perhaps in many ways, diminished the more distant and detached realm of the internet and VoiceThread [multimedia slideshows created by participants in order to share their curricular and student work with colleagues online]. Had the participants not been exposed to such rich, personal, face-to-face experiences, we may have seen VoiceThread being used in a more active and enthusiastic way."[7] We need more of this kind of discussion in the book and in general. It is far more provocative and useful than a myriad of examples where everything seems to unroll as designed. How do we make the online conversation just as lively as the one where we are all in the same room? What *is* the solution to the dilemma described?

The final section of the book, "Building Something New," lives up to its chapter title. Here Crow and Din explore how the very nature of collaboration changes in its online manifestation, "...through its ability to document and archive all our interactions, process-artifacts, and creations..." unlike the in-person counterpart. Online collaborative learning "...invites us to constantly re-visit and re-examine our creations, not only as individuals, but also as a community."[8] We can evaluate exactly how we move through a project from its inception throughout its many iterations, revisions, and applications. We don't just have the results; we have the road map.

In the "Art21 and Professional Development" case study, Jessica Hamlin hits the nail on the head when she admits that even after years of offering workshops to teachers "...how little we knew about the impact of our work in the classroom." The traditional forms of workshop evaluation still could not capture the ways in which the workshop material was being used over time: "...there was a sense of frustration about how difficult follow-up and follow-through was with this pro-fessional development format."[9] *A-men!* Online collaborative learning gives us a chance to address this endemic problem as workshop participants interact with both their students and the museum educators throughout the time that they are trying out new ideas at their schools. The constant feedback enriches the project and ensures that the workshop component is not the end point of the tie between museum and classroom educators. The curricular material generated during a workshop is continually being adjusted and adapted by all workshop alumni in the ongoing online community of co-teachers/co-learners. The classroom teachers gain a real sense of involvement and investment in the project, and the museum people have a chance to see how their work is applied in a school setting. This goes a long way toward solving a big problem that has been the subject of much discussion amongst museum colleagues: the inability to provide funders with solid evidence about the ways in which our museum resources are being used in the class.

The very last chapter of the book is perhaps most helpful of all. It is a conver-sation, recorded after the first summer of a workshop integrating technology before, during and after the sessions. Here representatives of the partnering in-stitutions — the Metropolitan Museum of Art and the American Museum of Natural History — talk directly and honestly about challenges faced, choices made, and the results of their decisions. The conversation is particularly in-structive and thought-provoking because it gives us an unflinching insight into the process of online collaboration, tracing the development of a project and chronicling both progress and pitfalls. (After all, this is a book for museum edu-cators, not a manual for public relations staff!)

Here Crow explains the need to have "connecting threads" to provide co-hesion in a program that looks at art in a science museum and science in an art museum. The idea of "inquiry" became one of those key threads, a central, unifying focus.[10] Participants in the conversation examine the use of the common online space as a tool for planning and revision. They talk about the comfort of having a blended program; some teachers feeling freer to express themselves in onsite sessions, others through online forms of communication. The conversation touches on the differences in how people interact face-to-face and online, and the ways in which the online relationships being built make the face-to-face encounters a richer experience. This in turn contributes to a deeper extended relationship afterward when people are back to classrooms, offices, and the online version of their interchanges.

The character of online collaboration — the ways in which the online experience affects outlooks, outputs, and outcomes — is a fascinating area of study. It is not an analysis of the technological tools at our disposal, but rather an inquiry into *how* we work together with those tools. In the skilled hands of William Crow and Herminia Din, it becomes a way for us to think through and apply our knowledge of online and in-person behavior, as well as our perceptions of individual expectations and group dynamics, to the life-cycles of our own projects.

Notes

1. Crow, William B. and Herminia Wei-Hsin Din. *All Together Now: Museums and Online Collaborative Learning* (Washington, DC: AAM Press, 2011), 7.
2. Ibid., 20.
3. Ibid., 39.
4. Ibid., 58.
5. Ibid., 79.
6. Ibid., 95.
7. Ibid., 99.
8. Ibid., 109.
9. Ibid., 112.
10. Ibid., 127.

About the Reviewer

Jayne Gordon is the Director of Education and Public Programs at the Massachusetts Historical Society. MHS education department websites such as "The Coming of the American Revolution" (funded by the National Endowment for the Humanities) and "The Case for Ending Slavery" (funded by the Library of Congress) are centerpieces for online, onsite, and blended learning programs for teachers and students.